BOARD DEVELOPMENT

Maximizing the Impact of Your Nonprofit or Church Board of Directors

Roger Dill

Jazz Business Consulting

Heartbeat Division

I have been the beneficiary of working with some great governance boards, as well as discouraged by those who saw their board membership as an opportunity to wield their weight as a personal fiefdom.

In this comprehensive work, Roger Dill has assembled an encyclopedic knowledge of how boards shouldoperate in service to an organization's purpose, mission, and strategic goals. For some, this will be a "Gentlemen/gentleladies, this is a football" moment. For some, it will be an education on how to have respectful, spirited discussions, often with crucial conversations being the result. For some, it will be an affirmation that the good-hearted and good-headed folks serving your organization can rest assured that you are on the right track. But without some self-assessment, how will you know?

Filled with useful anecdotes and examples of what's helpful or disruptive, Board Development carefully navigates the space between the roles of a governing board and its senior staff leadership. A careful definition of that space will determine a board's effectiveness or dysfunction.

The Heartbeat Division of Jazz Business Consulting seeks to serve those who are passionate about making their organization have a great "vibe," a combination of clarity, competency, and chemistry. I found the sections on "Running Better Meetings" and one of the many helpful Appendices, "Making Meetings Matter," alone worthy of using this book for your Board's development and self-reflection.

- **Rev. Dr. R. Kevin Murphy, retired senior leader and adjunct seminary associate professor of leadership and homiletics**

BOARD DEVELOPMENT

Contents

Pre-Introduction

The conductor is the only one who doesn't play an instrument but is responsible for how the music sounds.

    - Barry Jenkins, the creator, director, and producer of *The Chosen*, the first-ever multi-season show about the life of Jesus of Nazareth.

IN THE QUOTATION ABOVE, Barry Jenkins is not referring to a nonprofit or church congregation board of directors. But his comment could just as well apply to one.

Consider that a vibrant group of men and women wisely oversees their particular organization, but they do not typically oversee day-to-day operations. They don't get involved in the organization or congregation's programs. They don't attend staff meetings. They don't clean up after events. There are many activities they don't do.

In that way, the board of directors is the only performer that doesn't play an instrument. Yet, how they provide oversight for the organization will significantly influence how their "music" sounds.

I've written this book to help boards of directors function better and to provide oversight, encouragement, resources, and support for the senior leader they select to run their organization.

The metaphor I will use throughout the following pages will suggest that a board should operate more like a jazz ensemble or orchestra than a corporate entity. If you prefer the latter, don't read any further. You will only be frustrated.

But suppose you believe that a board overseeing a faith-based nonprofit or church congregation should possess relational strength without sacrificing its clarity and competency. In that case, I think you will like what you read.

Pastor Craig Groschel says, "Everyone wins when the leader gets better." It is also true that, "An organization wins when its board gets better." Better board leadership and oversight leads to better organizational music. It is also what your organization and the people it serves deserve.

Section One
The Power of Vibe

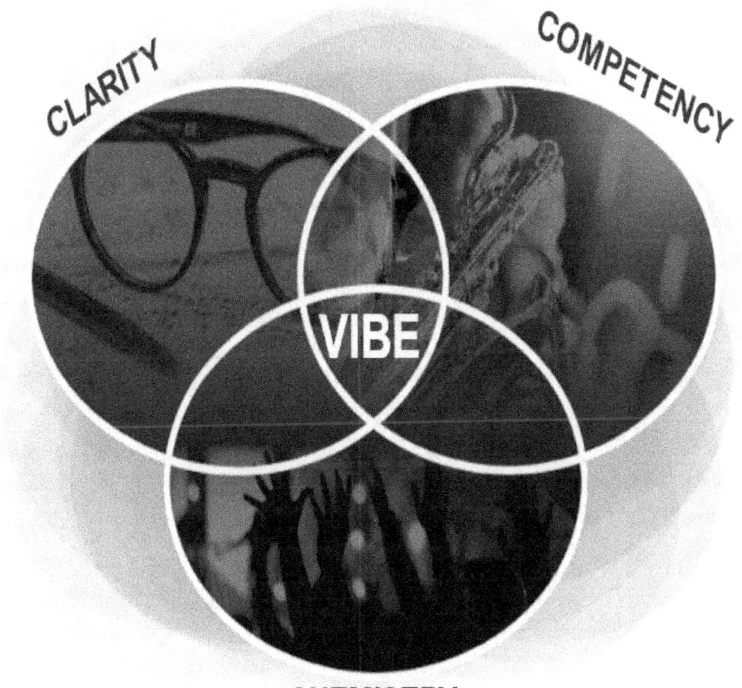

Vibe Model

Introduction
Failure

A man must be big enough to admit his mistakes, smart enough to profit from them, and strong enough to correct them.

    - John Maxwell.

I DON'T LIKE TO FAIL. I would never have written this book if it weren't for a particular failure as a board member overseeing a vital non-profit youth organization.

There are many maxims attached to the subject of failure, including:

"Failure is not final."

"Failure is a great teacher."

"Failure isn't fun!"

I got my first taste of failure as a ten-year-old Little League baseball player with aspirations of replacing my childhood hero, Mickey Mantle. I came up in the bottom of the last inning with two outs and the bases loaded. We trailed by one run. I didn't imagine the New York Yankees would send a scout to watch me play; however, I was confident I could help win the game.

I struck out.

I felt the sting of failure so profoundly that I told my dad I wanted to quit. He responded, "You struck out. You failed to hit the ball. That doesn't make *you* a failure."

His logic was lost on me. With tears streaming down my face, I asked, "What's the difference?"

"That's up to you. We have practice tomorrow morning. I expect you to be there." My father was our team's coach.

"I don't want to do that," I mumbled.

"What do you want?" he asked.

"I want a do-over and get a hit!"

I showed up the following day, proving at least two of the above maxims correct: "Failure is not final" and "It still isn't fun!"

It wouldn't be the last time I experienced failure.

I have served on multiple boards in my adult life, some powerful and life-changing and some horribly dysfunctional. One glaring failure was the impetus to write this book about board development.

The primary role of a board is to provide oversight on behalf of its organization. However, when it came to leaning into generating the critical conversations needed to be successful, I struck out again!

Light in a Dark Place

In your imagination, come with me into East Oakland, California. The area has a sinister and dangerous reputation.

It is known for its high murder rate and is consistently in the nation's top ten most dangerous places. There are abnormally high rates of drug abuse, theft, and violence, and a reputation for being a city whose residential needs far outweigh its resources.

Within the scariest part of this city, there is a group of courageous, gritty, God-dependent youth leaders. They provide two programs for kids. One is for younger children; the second one caters to teenagers. If you walk into the chapel on a Friday night where the teen group meets, there is so much passion for the Lord, you wouldn't be sure if you were experiencing an earthquake or a youthquake!

The teen ministry was founded in the early 2000s to bring light into the darkness. This program fills a crucial need for young people because few Oakland churches offer youth programs.

I had the privilege of serving as the (interim) executive director for fifteen months and as a board member for five years. During my tenure, we had twenty-four full-time and part-time ministry staff.

The work was intensive.

We experienced enormous challenges, like scrambling to find enough Bay Area churches to help us stuff 40,000 plastic eggs for the annual Easter Egg hunt or when we needed help hosting an annual Christmas event for over 2,000 attendees. Those who came received gifts for their children; and for some, those were the only gifts they would get.

What I remember most is the sheer dedication of the youth staff team. They brought this passion to work daily. They were just kids, most of them in their early twenties. Today, I know it is popular to complain about the younger generation's work ethic. These young leaders exemplified everything good (and hopeful) about this country's next generation of leaders.

They did more than run programs or events. They engaged with hundreds of kids weekly and met with children, youth, and often with the parents. They took the kids to the local McDonald's or Starbucks and treated them to Happy Meals and Frappuccinos, often paying with the little money they earned. These courageous young leaders also provided a safe place for intimate conversations. It didn't matter if the kids were gangbangers, ex-addicts, or facing crazy challenges. Additionally, our leaders regularly made hundreds of weekly home visits to comprehend what the teens and children faced.

Many of these kids had no way of getting to gatherings and back home. Those same youth leaders became legally licensed bus drivers. That's right! Not only did they minister to them, but they also picked them up and took them home for every meeting.

Bad Leadership in a Good Ministry

The ministry's founder had a big vision. He wanted to "lead the city of Oakland to God!" Big dreams inspire young leaders. Our staff worked tirelessly and selflessly to provide whatever it could to bring the vision to life.

Unfortunately, there is a big gap between *telling* leaders to lead a city to God and equipping, resourcing, and empowering them to accomplish this significant challenge. Sadly, although our board of directors financially supported the work, we failed to oversee the youth ministry competently. We should have resourced these incredible leaders to do what they were capable of doing. Ultimately, our shortcomings became theirs. We lost good leaders as a result. Furthermore, my reluctance to lean into vital conversations in board meetings contributed to that failure. I wrote this book based on my disappointing experience.

Every nonprofit organization and church congregation deserves the oversight of a board of directors comprised of vibrant and committed board members. Had I been more courageous, the young leaders could have accomplished even greater things!

You can't let your failures define you. You have to let your failures teach you.
- President Barack Obama.

The founder served as the chairperson of the board of directors. He was a visionary whose idea of leadership development was not so much, "I do, and you help," but rather, "I tell, and you do." If he wanted your opinion, he would give it to you.

I began to see him as a dominating and manipulative leader.

His dreams and vision were in ample supply, and he had a pipeline of available young leaders. They came equipped with enormous energy, passion, and willingness to do whatever it took to succeed. I watched him take advantage of their willingness in a self-serving way.

I spent fifteen months in the interim position. I sat in on weekly meetings where he continued disparaging the young leaders, criticizing them for missing small details and treating them in demeaning ways. He did it all in the name of "coaching."

For all his perceived talents and vision, the founder possessed another Achilles' heel. He would not play nicely with others, particularly leaders of area churches who partnered with our ministry. I first noticed it when fewer and fewer senior leaders in Oakland participated in our outreach events. Additionally, my relational network in the area gave me a consistent message. They informed me, "We love what the ministry is doing. We think so highly of all the youth leaders. We cannot work with your founder."

It also took me a while before I realized that the founder/board chair wanted something other than an executive director. He didn't want a leader in the role. He didn't want my insights; he wanted fundraising from my network.

I tenured my resignation but stayed on as a member of the board of directors.

I observed him treating several of the board members with the same disrespect. His chief target was the board treasurer, who received his fury simply because he did not like the financial reports the treasurer submitted. It was the perfect example of someone "shooting the messenger."

I look back on this ministry and ask myself, "Why wasn't I stronger? Why did I neglect my oversight responsibilities?" In my honest appraisal, I valued harmony over accountability. I didn't want to be the guy shouting, "The emperor has no clothes," even as he sat "naked" through one board meeting after another.

Thinking my presence could protect our young leaders, I was blind to the reality that I wasn't willing to challenge the board chairperson openly. I didn't want to be the troublemaker and the one to say confrontational and uncomfortable things. I also knew some board members were moved by the chairperson's manipulative charisma, charm, and energetic passion. I figured if I challenged him openly, it could split the board. Such an outcome would make performing even more difficult for our young leaders.

One morning during our monthly board meeting, the board chair informed us that the two co-senior leaders of the youth ministry were being replaced. I quietly began to recall the number of senior leaders we had who were no longer a part of the ministry. I realized nine senior or co-senior leaders had resigned or been fired in ten years.

I pointed this out to the rest of the board. The founder shrugged his shoulders and said, "Not everyone has the same leadership style. Some don't appreciate how I lead."

I took a chance.

I told him I was one of those who was not a fan of his authoritative leadership style. He glanced around the room, looking for any sign that I had support from anyone else. No one said anything.

I read the room. I was not necessarily alone in my opinion about his leadership style but I was in my willingness to assert that our young leaders deserved better.

I realized I was correct about the existing culture of fear. It became clear that I could not make a difference. I resigned shortly after the meeting.

I share my experience because I still regret not having a positive impact on those youth leaders. I should have fulfilled my oversight responsibilities as a board member.

My personal failure was two-fold.

First, I confused giving the founder/board chair credit for birthing the ministries and its accomplishments with giving him the authority to act autonomously without accountability. Serving as the founder and board chair allowed him to grab and use power not given to him in the founding documents. Because I was aware, I should have challenged him in private over his overreach. Instead, I ignored his weaknesses and made excuses for his toxic behaviors.

He serves as a prime example of a board member stretching into the day-to-day operation of the ministry. To make matters worse, he quickly blamed others whenever the organization experienced setbacks. No one was safe from his critical spirit. Looking back, I wish I had addressed his toxic behavior by challenging the fear-based culture he was creating.

Second, I should have addressed how his siloed leadership style negatively impacted the staff working so hard to bring his vision to life. The mission suffered because other Oakland leaders would not engage with us to accomplish more together than we could do alone. This created a heavier weight to bear on the part of our young leaders.

Back then, I imagined I was honoring him by not addressing my concerns, first in private or, if that failed, openly in a board meeting. I convinced myself that I would not be the cause of disunity.

There are many things I told myself.

Here is what I would like to tell those youth leaders. "I'm sorry for failing you. I should have met your passion with the courage to speak up. I should have been better."

I hope my insights can serve you well.

If you serve on a board of directors or work for a non-profit organization, this book will bring you great relief. You will find simple, easy-to-apply tools to avoid the heartache of dysfunction, distrust, and destruction of your dreams and aspirations to make the world better.

Clarification of Terms

It could be cumbersome to use various terms to describe what is a reference to the same position or group (i.e., I will use the term "senior leader" to describe what some organizations or denominations would refer to as CEO, president, priest, lead pastor, etc.). I will also use gender pronouns interchangeably. This is not a statement about the theology of whether a woman is permitted to serve as a pastor or as an elder. In full disclosure, I think women bring tremendous value to these roles.

Term **(As typically used** **in the book)**	Used Interchangeably With (or used to describe)
"Board of Directors"	Used interchangeably with "council, vestry, board of elders, session."
"Members"	Used interchangeably with "directors, elders, presbyters, etc."
"Chairperson"	Used interchangeably with "president, head elder, warden, etc.)
"Organization or Faith-Based Organization"	Used to describe "nonprofit organizations" and "church congregations" alike

"Senior Leader"	It describes the Chief Executive Officer, Executive Director, President, Senior or Lead Pastor, Rector, Priest, etc.
Use of Pronouns	Pronouns such as he, she, him, or her will be used at different times in the book, understanding that any could be used in the sentence.

Chapter 1
The Nonprofit Nation

It's a sin to bore a kid!
- Jim Rayburn

It's a sin to bore a board member!
- 2023 Paraphrase

IN 1939 IN GAINESVILLE, TEXAS, a Presbyterian minister hatched an idea to hire a part-time seminary student and give him the job description to "go hang out on the local high school campus and get to know the kids." Jim Rayburn was that student, and he couldn't have imagined a better job than the one handed to him. Neither the pastor nor Jim imagined what would become of the organization they called Young Life. By 2019, Young Life had clubs in 8,513 high and middle schools, with an average weekly attendance of 369,600 teens. In addition, it numbered over 55,000 volunteers and 5,702 paid staff members. Another 241,242 teens participated in Young Life's robust camp programs. One of the metrics they continue to track is "kids known by name." At last count, they knew 1,058,067 students by name. It is little wonder Young Life is known for being a relational organization!

Young Life is a beautiful example of what is best about nonprofit faith-based organizations.

The State of the Nonprofit World in America

Nonprofit organizations, including over 300,000 individual church congregations, do not always receive recognition and gratitude for the difference they make in American communities and abroad.

As of 2019, there were 1.54 million nonprofit organizations in America. A little over one-third of them are faith-based.

The nonprofit world is impressive. It accounts for five percent of the US economy, with approximately 2.62 trillion dollars of combined revenue. Those nonprofit organizations oversee $5.99 trillion in assets.

Furthermore, the nonprofit world is the third-largest employment industry, accounting for 1.9 million employees. Each of the top one hundred nonprofits reports over $150 million of income annually, and the top eleven organizations all claim over $1 billion in yearly revenue.

Imagine if all the nonprofits were their own country. It would represent the fifth largest economy in the world.

Fortunately for all these organizations, the American public is generous. Some 175 million Americans donate to at least one nonprofit annually. Not just financially, either. People also give their time. In 2017, one out of four Americans volunteered their time for nonprofits. According to research, the average volunteer gives 137 hours annually. That means the 1.54 million nonprofits received roughly nine billion hours of volunteer time.

There are trillions of revenue dollars and assets to manage and billions of hours of volunteer time provided to advance the causes of these vast numbers of organizations and congregations. These causes are impressive, including, but certainly not limited to:

- Care for the elderly
- Support for under-resourced families and individuals
- Addressing illiteracy
- Immigration opportunities and issues
- Foster care initiatives
- Global water resource needs
- Treating diseases, especially in third-world countries
- Social justice causes, i.e., racism, discrimination, religious discrimination
- Supporting victims and families of cancer, Alzheimer's disease, heart issues, and autism
- Homelessness and hunger
- Prison inmate needs, including rehabilitation and reentry opportunities
- Alcohol and drug addiction recovery

Did I miss the one you care most deeply about? If so, it is because I merely scratched the surface of the enormous needs in our world, many of which are addressed by nonprofits and congregations. Their adopted causes bring safe haven, hope, and healing to those they serve. Many of these nonprofits don't simply supply a handout; they offer a hand-up! As a result, lives are not just touched. Many are saved... some forever!

Let's Not Forget the Board of Directors

One last nerdy fact is that each nonprofit is overseen by its own board of directors. Imagining each board comprises an average of five members and meets every month, nearly one-hundred million hours of mostly volunteer time are provided to oversee all of these nonprofits and congregations. And that is only counting hours spent in meetings!

One of Jim Rayburn's favorite, often-quoted phrases was, "It's a sin to bore a kid!" I point this out because, in over 100 million hours of nonprofit board meetings, there are ample opportunities for BOARDom to creep into the boardroom.

So let me paraphrase Rayburn's comment: "It is a sin to bore a board member!"

With so much at stake, I have gained tremendous respect and appreciation for the individual board members who voluntarily give their time and often their financial resources to help oversee each nonprofit and church congregation.

I have witnessed firsthand the difference a wise and vibrant board makes in the success of an organization. When a board is enthusiastically engaged, everyone wins, especially those they serve.

However, I have also experienced the drag on an organization's progress and success when a board operates in an unhealthy manner or needs clarification about what is expected. It is painful to watch.

When people are part of a disengaged and ineffective board, the result is BOARDom (usually spelled boredom). "Boredom" is "a state of being weary and restless through the lack of interest." BOARDom on the other hand is a waste of one of the most significant resources a nonprofit possesses, its people! And boredom robs people of their curiosity and creativity and limits them from reaching their utmost potential. When people don't reach their potential, neither does the organization they serve. BOARDom ensues and it finds its way into the board room for several reasons, including:

- Board members are losing sight of what is at stake in their organization.

- Too many board members cannot describe the organization's mission. (Perhaps there isn't one.)

- There is a lack of clarity on how success is defined. If a mission does exist, board members are unaware of "what the score is." (The score, in this case, is a simple way to report the progress made relative to the missional intentions of the organization.)

- The only contribution expected from a board member is to write a check. If such is the case, eventually, astute directors figure out that "one need not be present to give."

Long-term BOARDom usually leads to half-hearted efforts, and then to disengagement. G. K. Chesterton once said, "There are no uninteresting things, only uninterested people." With so much at stake, one cannot afford to be an "uninteresting" board member.

BOARDom Does Not Belong in the Boardroom!

Trillions of dollars to oversee, billions of volunteer hours contributed, and millions of volunteer hours of board directors' time are provided to advance the causes of the vast number of nonprofit organizations and church congregations. It's impressive.

When I chose the title for this book, I intended to avoid developing boredom. Boredom does not require development. It unintentionally exists, and it may be damaging.

Boredom is the mold of the boardroom world. Just as mold spores grow in places with excessive moisture, boredom grows in areas with a surplus of confusion, frustration, purpose-absent gathering, domineering personalities, or the lack of progress on one's mission.

Treating boardroom BOARDom is a lot like trying to get rid of mold. If you Google "how to eliminate mold," over 12 million articles will appear in less than two seconds. If you Google "how to eliminate boredom," over seven-and-a-half million suggestions pop up. Also included are millions of tips for how to treat each one.

When it comes to treating mold, the top suggestion involves using bleach. However, if you read other articles, you will discover that bleach can assist mold to grow and spread. There are successful ways to treat mold, but it can find a way to return.

There is a definite way to treat BOARDom. The theme of this book is that every nonprofit organization and church congregation deserves the oversight of a board of directors comprised of vibrant people to ensure its sustainability and maximize advancing its mission.

The best way to alleviate boredom is by preventing its presence in the first place. That starts with knowing what type of board you want to build. Remember, your organization deserves an exceptional board of directors. I did not say "should have" or "might be fortunate to get," but it deserves to have a board comprised of vibrant people.

I have deliberately chosen to use the descriptive word vibrant. It is not that other descriptors, like competent, caring, wise, or willing, are not worthy choices. I want those qualities present as well. It is just that noteworthy vibrancy is often missing from board meetings.

Vibrancy is derived from the word vibe, which means "full of energy and enthusiasm, pulsating with life, vigor, or activity." It describes a person's emotional state or the atmosphere of a particular place "felt by others." Jazz musicians often claim their genre gave birth to the concept of vibe. They often use the term to describe a person, group, place, or experience as possessing or creating a particular emotion.

Vibe is vital to an organization's success and a deterrent to BOARDom as well.

BOARDom's Antidote

Vibe is the antidote not only to BOARDom, but also to the underperformance, lack of production, absence of motivation, and relational dysfunction that permeates nonprofit boardrooms in America.

Vibe can be uniquely experienced, and one person may enjoy a particular type of vibe while another might find it unpleasant. Yogi Berra once said about a specific restaurant in New York, "No one goes there anymore; it's too crowded." One might conclude that Yogi was not a big fan of the vibe of noisy, crowded eating establishments.

Whether you enjoy a particular vibe or not, you cannot deny its presence. Vibe is everywhere. Take a moment to reflect on the vibe of some common examples. What is the vibe of your favorite coffee establishment? Before Peet's Coffee and Starbucks came on the scene, the most anyone ever hoped for was a fresh cup of Joe. No one thought about the atmosphere, music, Wi-Fi connection, or ordering a Venti Caramel Ribbon Crunch Frappuccino.

What is the vibe of your dentist's office? I doubt there is enough laughing gas to make it feel like Disneyland. Speaking of Disneyland, what is its vibe? That's easy; it is "The Happiest Place on Earth."

Finally, in your opinion, what is the vibe of Congress? How about noxious, toxic, and thoroughly dysfunctional for starters?

When you attend a sporting event, you experience a vibe. The arena or stadium starts rocking when the home team makes a comeback because the collective vibe leads to momentum and results, like winning games. What kind of vibe do you experience when you attend and participate in your board of directors?

Wouldn't you like the board you serve on to obtain excellent organizational results? It begins with creating a noteworthy vibe.

A Story About Vibe and Prison

I must lead with a confession: I am not much of a connoisseur or fan of the flute. As a musical instrument, it isn't my preferred listening. And then I heard Roger Glenn play at the Louisiana State Penitentiary in the summer of 2009.

Roger was part of a group of musicians that spent a week at the prison grounds. Members of the Count Basie Jazz Ensemble, college professors, college students, worship pastors, and even one member of the Rock and Roll Hall of Fame. They gathered to play a jazz version of Johnny Cash's Folsom Prison concert. They came in response to an invitation from Jamie Davis, the former lead vocalist of the Basie Orchestra. Louisiana State Penitentiary is known as Angola Prison and was once one of the harshest prisons in America. Every Angola inmate serves a life sentence. I got to tag along to work with the inmates, even those on death row.

One evening, the musicians performed to a packed house of inmates in what Warden Burl Cain later called the "finest concert that the prison had ever hosted." The next afternoon the same performers played for many of the prison personnel and guards. Roger Glenn played his flute.

Roger was not even scheduled to perform. He was sitting in the audience listening to Lady Bianca, a Grammy-award nominated blues singer. She invited Jamie to join her in singing the Edwin Hawkins Singers' classic, "Oh Happy Day."

In typical jazz fashion, the song took many impromptu twists and turns, leading to several solos from the accompanying musicians. Roger was sitting four rows directly in front of me when suddenly he bolted from his seat and sprinted into a back room. When he reemerged, he was carrying a flute. He leaped onto the stage without an invitation and broke into an improvised solo. Roger performed with passion and flare, even tossing in some unrehearsed choreography.

That is a great vibe! You know vibe when you see, hear, or feel it. Good vibe and a bad vibe alike, but in Roger's case, he created an extra great one.

Roger Glenn's solo was part of a performance that led Warden Cain to invite the musicians back for an encore twelve months later. Those two events were filmed, recorded, and turned into a live album release entitled "Free on the Inside."

Similar experiences of great vibe inspired businessperson Sam Beler to start a nonprofit foundation that has done remarkable things in the lives of Hall of Fame jazz musicians and underserved students. Sam's Unity Music Foundation's mission is to provide scholarships for students who would not be able to pursue educational opportunities without financial aid.

The Unity Music Foundation has served under-resourced students and their families for over a decade. To this point, the foundation has provided over two hundred scholarships to students who have received the opportunity to attend colleges and study under incredible music professors because of what was birthed from the experience at Angola State Prison. Some recipients have graduated from institutions like the Juilliard School of Music.

Vibe is a Good Thing

Two years before the Free on the Inside performance at Angola Prison, a group of college professors and some students joined the Basie Jazz Ensemble at a recording studio in Los Angeles to produce Jamie's debut album entitled, It's A Good Thing, produced by Sam Beler. This is when and where my wife and business partner Jody Bagno and I were schooled about vibe's place of prominence in the jazz world.

The night before the album's debut at the San Francisco Palace of Fine Arts, Sam hosted a launch party at his home. The musicians who played on the album jammed into Sam's living room. Jody and I made the guest list.

Those attending the recording sessions in Los Angeles told remarkable stories. They shared how many musicians did not even know each other and had never played together. They recorded sixteen songs in two days; only two numbers required a retake – unheard of in the music industry!

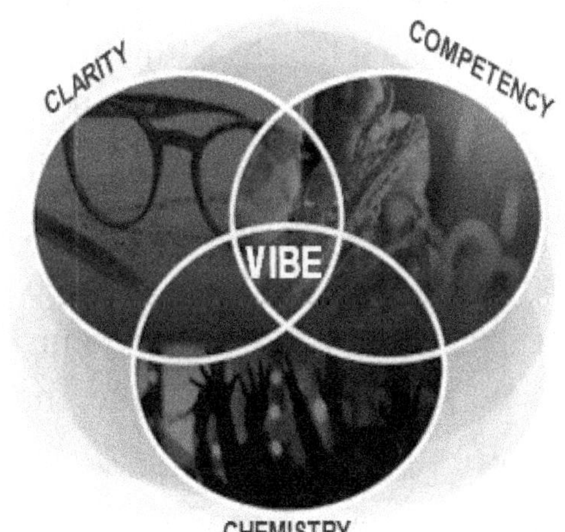

Vibe Model

The musicians attributed the recording's success to the presence of a "great vibe." One musician said, "The vibe was so thick that you could peel it off the wall!"

Hearing vibe referred to repeatedly as a primary contributor to the album's successful recording, Jody and I started asking everyone we met how they would define the word. The musicians loved talking about it.

We had some fascinating conversations, but one with Scotty Barnhart stood out. Scotty is the featured trumpet soloist with Basie, an author, a Florida State University professor, and a recording artist. (Currently, Barnhart is the Director of the Basie Orchestra.)

Scotty's definition was brief and to the point. He said, "Vibe happens when you bring together talented musicians who have mastered their instruments (competency). They are clear about the piece they are going to play and how they intend to play it (clarity). Finally, they have such great synergy and connection that with a nod of the head or a glance from the director, they know who will play the solo or when to wrap up the song (relationship chemistry). People do not come to our shows to hear us play the perfect notes. They come because of the way the music makes them feel. When the band produces a great vibe, the audience feels it!"

Scotty Barnhart used the word vibe to capture the secret sauce that allows a group of individuals to become a great team, or in this case, a great band making beautiful music. The combination of clarity, competency, and chemistry allows a group of leaders, musicians, or board members to become a high-performing, relationally healthy group simultaneously.

I interrupted Scotty and Jody's conversation to blurt out, "That's what we do for executive and leadership teams! We're like the jazz of the business world." Jody named our company Jazz Business Consulting later in the evening. In fifteen-plus years, well over a third of our clients have been nonprofit organizations and church congregations.

"Vibe is the uncanny, invisible energy that emerges from the combination of clarity, competency, and chemistry leading to noteworthy momentum and results."

We define vibe this way:

Vibe is the uncanny, invisible energy that emerges from the combination of clarity, competency, and chemistry leading to noteworthy momentum and results.

Do not mistake vibe for a soft, emotional add-on to a team or, in this case, to a board of directors or any other organization. Vibe is a behavioral competency that builds and maintains relational strength to enable a group of people to understand the direction an organization needs to take and possesses the capabilities and resources to execute the pursuit of its chosen path.

Pay attention to the vibe on your board. It will either empower your oversight ability or diminish how your senior leader and his or her staff and volunteers will experience your leadership. The staff and volunteers deserve your best. It is easier to provide that when crystal-clear clarity, exceptional competency, and strong relational chemistry flow from the board of directors.

I guarantee your board is known by the people, including your donors and supporters, for possessing a particular type of vibe. To be truthful, is your board more like Disneyland or our nation's congress? I'll bet you an Iced Brown Sugar Oat Milk Shaken Expresso you'd prefer the Disneyland comparison.

Chapter 2
The Kind of Board Every Nonprofit Organization Deserves

People don't come to our shows because we play the perfect notes. They come because of the way the music makes them feel.

- Scotty Barnhart, professor, musician, author, and director of the Count Basie Orchestra.

Give me vibe over perfection any day!

- Jamie Davis, Three-Time Grammy Nominated Vocalist.

I WAS A HANDFUL as a little boy. I was perpetually in motion, and I rarely stopped talking. To make matters worse for my mother, my family's church did not have a children's ministry. So, my poor mother had to try and manage my behavior challenges. Maybe that is why I only remember having fun at church twice before my teen years. And both times, I got in trouble.

It reminds me of a story I heard years ago about a mother trying to get her active four-year-old under control one Sunday morning in church. She pleaded for his cooperation.

When nothing worked, she bribed him before resorting to threats. Exasperated, she blurted out, "Sit down and be quiet."

He yelled back, "But it's boring!"

His mother screamed back, "It's supposed to be!"

Boredom is a major problem when someone is engaged in everyday work. BOARDom causes board members to be disengaged. There is one thing worse than a board member who quits and leaves a nonprofit or church. Worse than quitting and leaving is the one that quits and stays!

Serving on a board of directors for a nonprofit or a church congregation should not end with someone screaming, "But it's boring!"

In the previous chapter, you were introduced to the concept of vibe and the three components that comprise it. I cannot overstate how important it is not to confuse vibe with just possessing two of the three elements. Worse yet, it would be a mistake to confuse vibe for a feel-good relational feeling. It is a combination of clarity, competency, and chemistry, and your board will need to simultaneously master all of them to provide the type of oversight that your organization deserves.

The father of modern management, Peter Drucker, once said, "If you can measure it, you can manage it." But before you measure something, you have to define it. Scotty Barnhart gifted us with the vibe's definition. It can be a gift to your boardroom as well. Let me begin this section by looking at each of vibe's core components and how they apply to a board of directors.

The Components of Vibe

Clarity: a board of directors must possess clarity and agreement on certain core concepts around its organization's cause and where it is headed. These concepts include:

- "Why does the organization exist?" (Purpose)
- "Where" is the organization eventually headed? What impact on the world does it intend to make?" (Vision)
- "What" actions and activities does the organization needs to perform regularly to fulfill its purpose and achieve its vision?" (Mission)
- "When" are the deadlines for short-term goals and objectives important for the organization to fulfill?" (Short-term strategic plans)

A key responsibility for any board of directors is to ensure that the senior leader has the support, resources, and direction needed to execute the missional calling of the organization. There is a tremendous advantage when the staff and volunteers clearly understand the purpose, vision, and mission, and every person is aware of their role in helping the organization achieve them.

Many nonprofit boards, however, behave less like bandmates and more like audience participants. Instead of actively participating to support the senior leader as he or she directs the organization, these types of boards make decisions on behalf of an organization that they don't fully understand.

Competency addresses "how" to execute the mission and includes the skillset, knowledge, and resources needed to achieve what is most important to the organization. I can imagine how incredibly frustrating to know what song a band wants to play but lacks musicians capable of performing it. It is equally maddening when a nonprofit or church congregation knows what it wants to accomplish but does not possess the necessary personnel with the proper skill set, knowledge, and resources to achieve its goals. It is essential to have the right senior leader in place and to resource her with capable personnel, finances, and other resources to achieve critical objectives.

It is just as frustrating to employ great leaders with excellent skills and the aptitude to accomplish great things but who lack clarity around the organization's mission and short-term goals.

In either case, clarity without competency or competency devoid of clarity creates an organizational environment prone to developing relational discord and mistrust, leading to self-serving or self-protective behaviors.

Chemistry starts with the "who" question. To paraphrase author Jim Collins, building a high-performing board requires "getting the right people in the band and playing the right instruments."

We have had the privilege of working with hundreds of clients of various sizes and purposes. We have observed one universally true phenomenon. Companies, nonprofits, or church congregations that fail to overcome relational dysfunction and form a healthy social environment will underperform. The relational condition of an organization will either multiply its performance or divide it. It is the law of vibe.

A savvy board of directors pays close attention to the unity factor within the board and the organization. It doesn't sacrifice a harmonious culture as a substitute for apparent success. It will not throw away success to have a kumbaya feeling.

Vibe Starts at the Top

Every organization or group of people possesses a vibe. Furthermore, a board of directors can assess, measure, cultivate, and manage the particular kind of vibe it wants for itself and the organization it oversees. This approach can be a game changer regarding the organizational culture you wish to have.

Vibe starts at the top. As a result, it has a "trickledown" effect. In nonprofit organizations and churches, it begins at the board level. It flows through the senior leader, executive team, staff, and volunteers until it reaches the people served by the organization.

Vibe flows in every boardroom, and whether it feels like Disneyland or Congress depends on how the members function together. These organizations rely on their board directors to:

- "Master their instruments" in the form of skillfully and competently overseeing their organization to fulfill its purpose, advance its mission, and achieve its vision.

- "Be clear about the piece they are going to play and how they are going to play it." Every member knows why the organization exists, where it is headed, and the organization is aligned around its mission.

- "Enjoy great synergy and connection" – a focus on creating and maintaining healthy relationships and unity.

When a board of directors creates and maintains great vibe and has chosen the right Chief Vibe Officer to serve as its senior leader, it enjoys a considerable advantage when it comes to building peak level performance.

Taking a Closer Look at Young Life

I don't know your current situation. I am not aware of the kind of vibe you have in your organization. But I know what a good vibe and its counterpart look and feel like. When Young Life started over eighty years ago, it had the kind of vibe teenagers liked. (It still does!)

When Young Life started, no one foresaw what it would become. Jim Rayburn was a young seminary student hired by Clyde Kennedy and assigned to get to know and befriend high school students. The pastor told Jim, "Don't worry about the kids that are already coming to church. I'll take care of them. You just hang out at the local high school."

As Jim got to know the teens, he invited them to meet with him in the pastor's office one night a week and to pray for kids at the school to attend their Young Life club. One night, one of the kids prayed for the football team captain to attend. As it happened, the captain's girlfriend was there. She guaranteed to have him at the next meeting. By then, over 70 high school students were attending this brand-new parachurch ministry designed for unchurched kids.

The captain came and he started bringing other football players. Shortly after attending his fifth meeting, the captain gave his life to Jesus.

The player's name was Burr Nichols. Later in the fall, Burr was killed in a tragic automobile accident. His parents asked Jim to officiate at the memorial.

Burr's dad told Jim that he was the only preacher his son would listen to.

Jim Rayburn started a full-fledged nonprofit ministry when he was still in grad school. He started it for kids just like Burr Nichols. Jim later wrote that Burr was like a lot of high school kids. They just needed someone to take an interest in them and share the Gospel in a relatable way. "The problem is," Rayburn said, "too many of them have never heard the Story." Then Jim finished his thought, "And I can't stand that!"

Jim Rayburn's life was fueled by a love for high school students who had never heard the Story. If you were to sit on the Young Life board, you would be well aware of its mission and vision.

- Young Life's Mission: "To introduce adolescents to Jesus Christ and help them grow in their faith."
- Young Life's Vision: "Together we have set our eyes Forward, joining in a movement that compels us to go deeper in our walk with Jesus while helping young people grow deeper in their

faith, to welcome a diverse team of men and women to all levels of leadership, to innovate new ways to reach and teach, and to grow – building relationships with more young people all over the world."

If you've ever had the privilege to know Young Life leaders, you immediately recognize how much they resemble Jim Rayburn. They love teenagers, and they love hanging out with them. They also know they must "earn the right to be heard" if they want to be influential.

How is Young Life doing? It has been nearly 85 years since Jim started the first Young Life club in Gainesville. According to the Barna Group:

- 4.9 million U.S. adults decided to follow Jesus in Young Life as students and are still practicing their faith today.

- 5% of pastors are Young Life Alumni.

- 11 million adults credit Young Life as the primary influence in developing their faith, and another 3.2 million acknowledge the ministry as one of the main influences in developing their faith.

- Alumni report that 22% say their faith was important to them before participating in Young Life. Today, 85% of alumni say their faith is very important.

- Just this past year, Young Life raised over $100 million more than the previous year (most of it aimed to expand its camp programs).

Those facts only apply to the United States. Today, Young Life operates in over one hundred countries worldwide.

I doubt Jim Rayburn or Pastor Clyde Kennedy saw that happening. What about the organization on whose board you sit? How do you know it won't have the same impact decades from now? Do you imagine it might not take decades to influence the lives of those you are serving currently? It is safe to say that Rayburn and Young Life grew into their vision. But the mission that started with kids like Burr Nichols hasn't changed. Young Life leaders know there are some kids who have never heard the story about Jesus. Just like Jim, "They can't stand it!"

The Board of Directors Vibe Assessment
What is the Vibe of Your Board of Directors?

Repeating Peter Drucker, "If you can measure it, you can manage it."

Our company has developed a way to measure the vibe of a nonprofit or church board. We call it our Board Development Assessment. It comes with an individualized report and exercises to address and improve a board of directors' clarity, competency, and relational chemistry. In the back of this book is an abbreviated version of the assessment you can take to get a feel for the vibe level on your board.

Our growth strategies and executive coaching company offers a more robust board assessment and report. To access it and other helpful materials and services, please visit http://jazzbc.com/jazz-heartbeat.

Go to our website at http://jazzbc.com/jazz-heartbeat/ to learn more about the complete assessment and other resources that we provide.

Section Two
Clarity

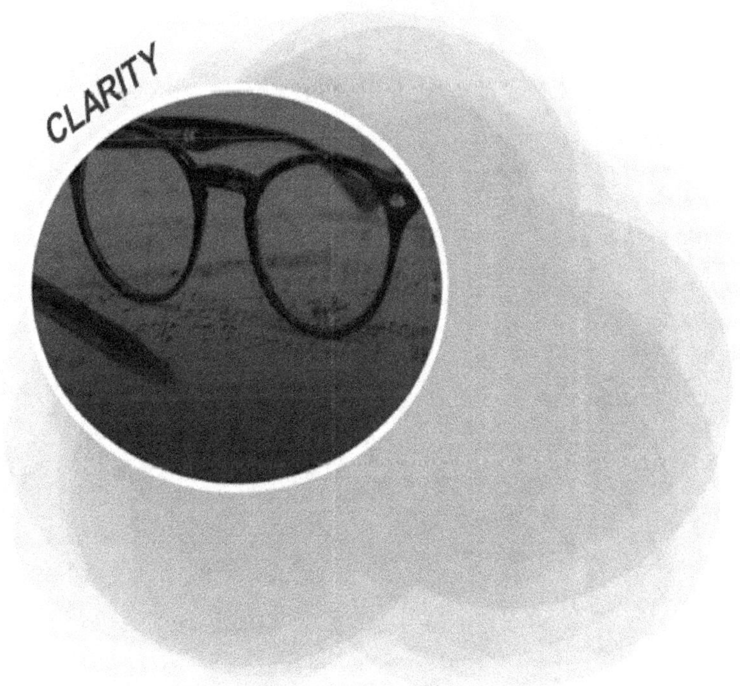

Vibe Eclipse Model

Chapter 3
Clarity Matters!

There are few things more powerful than a life lived with passionate clarity.

- Erwin McManus.

One of the primary functions of the brain is to act like a security system. When personal safety is threatened, the brain goes into fight or flight mode. Our brains stay hyper-aware of our surroundings and pay special attention to anyone or anything threatening our safety.

To remain alert, one's brain avoids burning unnecessary calories. Whenever your brain endures boredom, confusion, or unproductive mental activities, it goes into autopilot mode to conserve energy. (Think about how your laptop goes into sleep mode when not in use.)

When your brain is trapped in a boring board meeting, it must conserve enough energy to recognize any threat or emergency. After all, one never knows when a skunk might wander into the conference room.

Nothing burns calories like confusion. Confusion goes by several names: uncertainty, indecision, bewilderment, or perplexity. Regardless of what you call it, it dulls one's mental capacity. The antidote to confusion is clarity.

I have participated in enough board meetings to be convinced that board members sometimes have different perspectives about issues, challenges, roles, or decisions. I become excited when such diversity of opinion is present. It makes for a lively meeting except when those differing viewpoints are regarding an organization's primary mission. This is the one area where there must be complete agreement and alignment. In addition, I am no longer surprised when everyone on a particular board cannot explain the organization's mission. When this happens, confusion reigns, and brains strive to preserve calories.

There are times when confusion is inevitable and can be harmless. But being confused about the organization's mission is not benign. It leads to damaging results.

I watched a nonprofit organization suffer needlessly through a painful transition period, partially over having lost its missional focus. One senior staff member reported to the board of directors that he felt the staff team was confused by the CEO's lack of mission focus. The disgruntled staff member told the board, "He chases one shining object after another. No one is certain what we're working on, or if they know, they don't know why."

The senior staff member and the organization's CEO had once been friends. However, the staff member didn't let friendship stand in the way of a good power struggle. He even accused the CEO of misappropriating funds (which turned out to be completely false).

I will spare you the details. After several board conversations without the CEO being present, the board relieved him of his title and authority and made him Emeritus CEO. This turned out to be the first step in gently removing the CEO, who was also the founder, from the nonprofit.

I knew the CEO and the organization well. There was a lot of truth in what the senior leader said, especially about chasing shining objects. The CEO didn't regularly keep the mission in front of the staff team or the board. This allowed others to "fill in the blanks" and share their own missions.

Other board members did not know what the mission was – neither did the accusing senior leader. These realizations emerged when the newest board member asked for clarity regarding the mission statement. She was appalled when no one could tell her, including the senior staff person.

She later told me, "I was confused. After all, what is the difference between a senior leader who did not advance the mission and another who could not tell me what it was? When I discovered that the rest of the board did not know what it was, I knew this was not where I wanted to invest my time." She resigned shortly after the meeting.

One of the biggest differentiators between an organization consistently advancing its mission and one stuck in the mud is how well the leaders understand what they are trying to accomplish.

Clarity in Four Parts

Scotty Barnhart described one of vibe's elements as being "clear about the piece you are going to play and how you intend to play it." Nonprofit organizations and church congregations must possess the same clarity to make a meaningful difference in their community and the world.

Organizational clarity addresses purpose, vision, mission, and short-term strategic plans. Let us begin with purpose.

Purpose

Why does your organization exist? "Why" questions are often found in a college philosophy class, as in, "Why do we exist?" You will find significant value in asking and answering the question, "Why does our organization exist?" According to Guy Kawasaki in his book The Art of the Start, purpose is about making meaning. Kawasaki states that there are several ways an organization can make meaning in the world, including:

- Make the world a better place.
- Increase the quality of life.
- Right a terrible wrong
- Prevent the ending of something good

Consider your organization. What is the purpose it is trying to fulfill? Why did someone take the time to file the laborious paperwork with the IRS and the State Franchise Tax Board to give birth to its existence? Launching a nonprofit organization is as complex as starting a new business. Are you aware of the intentions of your organization's founder(s) and what inspired the birth of the nonprofit?

Has the original purpose changed? Has it evolved over time?

Let's return to the story of Young Life's beginning. The "why" of Young Life is observed in the frustration of Jim Rayburn. As he got to know the teenagers at the high school in Gainesville, Texas, Jim realized they had not given up on God, but they could not relate to how God was presented and represented in many local churches. Jim realized the kids needed a place to be befriended and loved. He saw there weren't enough options for teens to learn about Jesus in a way that made sense to them.

Jim's frustration is represented by his straightforward statement, "I can't stand that!" Embedded in Rayburn's vexation and passion for reaching unchurched teens, he discovered the reason, the cause, and his "why" to launch a ministry that, over eight decades later, still embodies the same driving purpose today. In addition to the 8,500-plus clubs in America, Young Life has partnered with like-minded and like-purposed people to extend its reach to over 100 countries today.

Young Life is a wonderful example of what knowing your purpose can do for the organization you help oversee.

Vision

Vision is a compelling and inspiring picture of the future. It is the eventual "where" or intended destination for an organization. Word pictures capture it best. The best example of vision in the 20th century was the "I Have a Dream" speech by Dr. Martin Luther King Jr. He did not use a word picture; he used an entire photo journal!

Dr. King spoke of government checks "stamped: insufficient funds." He imagined a "table of brotherhood" in the Red Hills of Georgia and an "oasis of freedom" in Mississippi. He emphasized the "content of one's character" more than the "color of one's skin." Finally, Dr. King envisioned "little white boys and girls holding hands and playing with little black boys and girls" in the racially turbulent state of Alabama.

Even today, images form in my mind when I listen to King's speech. He was not only a skilled orator and a gifted preacher, but Dr. King was also a profound painter of imagery. He used words instead of oils and canvas.

Visions inspire. They are compelling. They motivate team members. But there are not necessarily a lot of word picture painters these days.

Visionary leaders are few, a significant reason leaders "borrow" from visionaries. It is too bad because vision, like purpose, can get people up in the early morning, ready to do whatever it takes to help the organization advance its cause.

I remember when the nonprofit ONE launched and announced its vision. It wanted to see poverty end in this generation's lifetime. The vision causes people to imagine what a poverty-free society would look like. That is what compelling visions can do.

Mission

Not every nonprofit or church crafts a vision statement, and fewer describe their purpose. A higher number can explain their mission.

If the purpose is the starting line and vision is the finish line, then the mission is the road an organization follows to "run the race with perseverance" to fulfill its purpose and achieve its vision.

Purpose addresses the "why" question. Vision answers the "where" question. The mission focuses on the "what" question, as in what we will do consistently to advance the organization's cause. A significant cause of confusion in a boardroom is the lack of an agreed-upon mission that aligns everyone in the organization.

Short-Term Strategic Plans

Jesus the Strategist

One final component regarding organizational clarity is how an organization develops and addresses short-term planning. I have had plenty of encounters with nonprofit executives and clergy who look at me as if I have used foul language when I mention the word "strategy."

This is often a source of conflict the senior leader has with her board members, especially if it is a church board. The typical complaint from the senior leader is that the board focuses too much on finance and "business" issues, spiritual code language for "my board is too secular." At the same time, the typical lament from a board member is that the senior leader concentrates too little on the business or financial health of the organization, business code language for "our senior leader is too spiritual."

It makes it difficult for the senior leader and the board to find common ground to plan for short-term goals and objectives designed to help implement the organization's mission.

Jesus was strategic! To emphasize what I mean, let's go back to the very beginning of Jesus' ministry in the Palestinian region where he was born and raised. To set the stage, John has recently baptized Jesus. One might think Jesus would use the event to launch into his ministry. Instead, Jesus does what he often does; he disappears at the height of early public curiosity. He spends forty days alone in the desert, where the devil tempts him.

As we pick up the story, Jesus has journeyed to his hometown of Nazareth. He enters the local synagogue and is asked to read a passage from the prophet Isaiah. As Jesus reads, the assembled hear the Jewish Messiah's mission statement:

> The Spirit of the LORD is on me because he has anointed me to proclaim good news to the poor. He has sent me to proclaim freedom for the prisoners and recovery of sight for the blind, to set the prisoners free, and to proclaim the year of the LORD's favor.

Luke goes on to describe what happens next. Jesus rolls up the scroll and returns it to the attendant. Every eye is fixed on him. Then, Jesus drops the mic: "Today this scripture is fulfilled in your hearing."

Jesus claims the Messiah's mission was his mission, not because Jesus is a disciple of the Messiah, but because Jesus is the Messiah!

Instead of a standing ovation or the crowd suddenly hoisting Jesus up on their shoulders and marching him victoriously through the streets of Nazareth, they lead him out to a cliff in an attempt to throw him off of it.

It's time to leave town, which coincides with launching his earthly ministry. Being strategically minded, Jesus heads out to the region of Galilee.

Galilee! So many things would suggest that the area should not be the center point of his earthly ministry. It doesn't have the significance of Jerusalem. It lacks the history of several other cities in Israel. Furthermore, it is a vast area to cover, and Jesus is a solopreneur. He has yet to gather one single follower.

It is difficult to understate the area's size. According to Josephus, the Galilean region had roughly 204 villages, towns, and cities. For the sake of clarity, I am going to refer to all of them simply as "towns." Jesus chooses a strategy to launch his ministry in an area where the "rabbi-to-town" ratio was 1:204!

At this point, I might be tempted to rethink the part of Jesus being strategic. Consider the challenges he faces. No cars, no trains, no planes. He cannot jump on a bus, hail a cab, or catch a Lyft. He does not have access to a cellphone.

The Internet and social media will not exist for almost two thousand years.

But instead of rethinking Jesus' strategic acumen, I will double down on it.

Phase One: During the first year of Jesus' mission, he appears to have been working on a short-term plan. As he passes through some of those 204 towns, he heals people, casts out demons, and preaches good news to the poor. He follows the Isaiah blueprint to the T for what he should do. He draws people to him. Some will follow him for a day. Some will stay a little longer. Others are in for the long haul. Jesus pays careful attention as he converses with them, observes them, shares meals with them, and gets to know them better. During the initial 12 to 18 months, Jesus spends time with the men who will later follow him more intimately. His focus is to observe, learn about them, and identify those he will call his Apostles. Eventually, Jesus climbs a mountain and prays all night. In the morning, he descends and "called his disciples to him." Hundreds gather. These are the same folks he addresses during the Sermon on the Mount.

Phase Two: In Phase Two, Jesus appoints twelve disciples to be his Apostles and spends the following year teaching, training, and developing them to execute the same mission. Where does he do this with them? The familiar towns of Galilee.

Twelve months later, Jesus deploys them in teams of two to go into the same towns. Peter, James, John, Andrew, Matthew, and the others heal the sick, cast out demons, and preach good news to the poor. The ratio had become a much-improved ratio of 6.204 – one pairing every thirty-four towns.

Phase Three: Jesus takes the next six months and prepares, develops, and deploys thirty-five more pairs of disciples to go to the same 204 towns in Galilee. The ratio shrinks to a manageable team of two disciples for less than five towns (1:4.9756, to be more precise). What are their responsibilities? I will give you one guess; my money is on you to figure it out. They execute the same mission Jesus was doing three years before – all alone.

Do not ignore Jesus' brilliance as a strategist. To grasp the size of an area, the entire San Francisco Bay Area has less than two hundred towns in it. Jesus reached an area with more cities in less than three years without modern transportation, modern means of communication, and an absence of an advertising campaign or social media. The closest thing Jesus had to an Uber was the donkey colt his disciples borrowed for him to enter Jerusalem for his final Passover. Furthermore, he didn't have a budget, paid staff, or buildings to meet in.

It makes one wonder whether we're very good at strategic thinking!

Room Enough for Planning and Prayer in the Same Boardroom

I know Jesus never spoke about possessing a plan, deadlines, or projections. He did reference "reaching my goal" (see Luke 13:32, 33). But like Steve Jobs once said, "You can't connect the dots looking forward; you can only connect the dots looking backward." Applying Job's discipline of looking backward, one can readily see how Jesus planned to reach the entire region of Galilee, and he used three short-term strategic plans to get there.

There is no spiritual/secular split regarding the ministry of Jesus. There is room for planning and prayer in a boardroom.

This chapter emphasizes the vibe component of clarity. Clarity is the antidote to confusion that causes our brains to burn calories needlessly and senselessly. Confusion causes leaders to become bored and bored leaders become disengaged.

Once a board member or an entire board remains disengaged for a significant period, it leads to adverse outcomes. Often, long-term disengaged board members quit and leave the organization. Depending on the skill set, the director's network, and the member's financial resources, it is an unnecessary loss for the organization.

Worse yet, the disengaged board member quits but stays in place. Refrain from letting yourself believe that is not a loss, not if he continues to come to meetings. According to the Gallup Organization, overwhelming evidence shows how disengagement is like a virus spreading throughout a team or an entire organization. It reduces the production and contribution of other team members and board directors. No one is immune from the effects of disengagement.

One way to avoid disengagement is to remind everyone at the board level of the organization's purpose, vision, mission, and short-term goals and objectives. Ensure everyone knows what is at stake and who is counting on you to hit your targets and execute the organization's mission.

There are other critical clarity issues for board focus, and these are addressed in the following chapter.

Chapter 4

Sour Notes – Unspoken Expectations and Unexplained Responsibilities

There is one thing that all boards have in common, regardless of their structure, they do not function.

    - Peter Drucker.

No one rises to low expectations.

    - Les Brown.

I LOVE TEACHING LITTLE kids how to play baseball. There is always laughter and much fun, even when there are a lot of dropped balls, errant throws, and more swings and misses than hits.

Teaching young children how to hit involves the discipline of repetition. Children stand at home plate, and the adult tries to hit their bats. Eventually, the adult enthusiastically yells, "Run out the next one." That is code for "run to first base." In my experience, two-thirds of all kids run as fast as they can... to third base.

When a child learns a new game, there is plenty of room for confusion. Studies about how adults operate in business demonstrate that business professionals do not fare much better. According to an article in Forbes Magazine, 65% of organizations have an agreed-upon strategy. In comparison, 14% of employees understand the strategy, leading to 10% of all organizations successfully executing the plan.

That is the adult version of "running to third base." The Forbes article demonstrates that many companies or organizations, including nonprofit or congregational boards of directors, are running in the wrong direction. This may be what the board governance author and expert John Carver had in mind when he wrote, "Boards are typically incompetent groups made up of competent people." Carver is not being harsh. He is being honest.

Clarifying Expectations

I am constantly amazed when some successful, savvy, and highly confident business leaders join a board of directors and immediately stop thinking like a business professional. They stop thinking about how they would tackle specific challenges if they were to occur in their business. Their problem-solving skills are stilted.

In truth, many board members need elucidation regarding what is expected of them. They also need clarity about their roles, responsibilities, and what authority they possess to address issues, challenges, and opportunities.

While organizational clarity deals with elements like purpose, vision, mission, and strategic plans, clarity also addresses issues like:

- The purpose of a board of directors

- The expectations that surround roles, responsibilities, and authority.
- The oversight responsibility for the execution of the organization's mission.
- Creating agreements in advance on how to overcome disagreements, conflicts, and discord within the board when they arise.

Let's begin by addressing the chief purpose of a board of directors.

The Purpose of a Board of Directors:

Does a nonprofit organization or a church congregation need to have a governing board? Is it a legal requirement? The short answer is yes.

The better question would be, what purpose does a board serve? A board of directors is a body of elected or appointed members who jointly serve and with one voice oversee the organization's legal and financial matters and the senior leader to ensure the organization executes its mission.

I want to emphasize the phrase, "who jointly serve and with one voice oversee..." Boards create problems when their members forget they operate as one entity. No individual member, officer or not, represents the entire board without the board's permission.

The primary function of a faith-based nonprofit or church board is to ensure that the organization advances its God-given mission. This clarifies how a board supports and supervises its senior leader, allocates its funding, finances, and assets, as well as making decisions regarding property, activities, and strategy.

Roles, Responsibilities, and Authority

What should an individual expect when it comes to roles he will play, responsibilities he will carry, and what authority will he have to fulfill his function as a board member?

Expectations Regarding Roles

A "role" is a position that an individual assumes within an organization, whether it is a company, a school, an athletic team, or a board of directors. Most individuals on the board serve as members. Some also serve as officers or even as committee members or leaders.

All board members serve in a fiduciary role. The word "fiduciary" comes from a Latin term meaning someone whose duty or obligation is to "act faithfully in the interest of another," even "at the cost to oneself." It is a legal term and refers to someone who, because of her position, has a responsibility to act primarily on another's behalf.

The term is sometimes erroneously applied exclusively to the management of money. It carries a much broader meaning.

Expectations Regarding Responsibilities

The board of directors is responsible for acting jointly on behalf of the organization and providing oversight for the contractual, financial, staffing, and mission implementation.

The board acts together to represent the organization, while individual members are accountable for fulfilling three primary fiduciary responsibilities

The Duty of Care requires that each board member is responsible for acting with "reasonable care" in the organization's best interest. This means that board members will give proper time, energy, prayer, effort, and attention enabling them to:

- Know and understand the stated mission of the organization.
- Be aware of the organization's affairs (activities, finances, needs, and opportunities).
- Make decisions and act responsibly on the organization's behalf.

Caring for the organization is acting like the board member is an "owner or shareholder" concerned about its overall health and success. It means the member will attend meetings, represent the organization in the community, oversee the property and contractual agreements, and pay close attention to its financial health to ensure that the organization is focused on fulfilling its mission.

The Duty of Obedience requires each board member to be familiar and in compliance with the organization's legal documents, including its:

- Articles of Incorporation
- Constitution and by-laws
- Applicable legal requirements
- Denominational requirements (if a church)

New board members should also be updated on past decisions and commitments made by previous boards. A current member cannot say, "I am not obligated or bound to a decision or promise made before my time of service." Present board members are morally obligated to uphold previous commitments made by boards preceding their terms.

This raises some questions. Do you have a copy of your organization's by-laws? Have you read them, and do you understand these documents? These questions are essential because a board member is responsible for knowing, understanding, and abiding by those documents.

Several years ago, I received an SOS call from a church board of elders asking if I would meet with their board and senior pastor to help them resolve a conflict. When I arrived for the meeting, I was escorted to a conference room where four tables had been set up in a square. On one side of the room sat the elder board. On another side of the room were the deacons and deaconesses. The lead pastor was at a table by himself. I was asked to take my place (all alone) at the last table. An awkward feeling permeated the room. I knew the church was experiencing some conflict. I had been recommended to assist them in regaining their relational equilibrium. My curiosity piqued, and my guard was up due to the vague way they described the issue at hand.

The first words spoken were, "According to our founding documents..." and we were off to the races. No one had to tell them that the division they were experiencing was not minor. Deep hurt preceded the relational turmoil by the looks on several of their faces. (I will come back to this scenario later in the book.) Something has likely gone wrong if someone references the constitution.

The Duty of Loyalty means that for every board member, the most crucial priority is advancing the organization's mission. The organization's health and mission trump everything, therefore, board members should not personally benefit from decisions made by the board.

If an individual director stands to benefit from a decision made by the board, he must alert the other members of a conflict of interest and recuse himself from the discussion of the matter and any vote about it.

To protect itself, every board of directors must have a carefully worded conflict of interest policy to which to refer and to follow should a potential dispute arise. There should be a conflict-of-interest section in the by-laws of the organization's constitution.

Such action will cover the legal qualifications, but moral obligations must also be considered. The duty of loyalty is not just about the X's and O's to be included in founding documents. One should also take into consideration other potential conflicts, including:

- Friendships
- Family ties
- Rivals
- Unresolved relational matters

Other issues can influence how a director may govern. Again, nothing should come before acting in the organization's best interest.

Expectations Regarding Authority

The board is only in existence when it comes together to meet in person or online and acts as one unit on behalf of the organization it serves. Trouble occurs when individuals grab authority not provided to him or her and/or when they are not in sync with the entire board. No one board member carries the authority that belongs only to the board itself.

Therefore, all directors must understand what the by-laws spell out regarding authority given to individual board members, including board officers.

Most constitutions spell out the roles and responsibilities of each board office. However, these documents rarely grant additional authority to these offices. Hence, a board chairperson, for example, serves to organize and facilitate effective board meetings, to lead the board in understanding and executing the organization's mission, to ensure support and supervision of the senior leader, and to guarantee the board oversees the strategic direction and financial health of the organization.

However, unless the board's founding documents bestow additional authority, the chairperson has the same voting power as anyone else, including the most junior member. She is not given an extra "half-vote" for being the chairperson, nor does she carry additional authority.

When addressing the question of aboard member's authority, the answer is simple: the board carries the authority to represent, oversee, and make decisions on behalf of the organization. Individual board members, including officers, only possess the power to act with the expressed permission granted by the board.

NOTE: For more information regarding the roles, responsibilities, and authority of the officers of a nonprofit board, please refer to APPENDIX F.

Organizational Mission

When it comes to understanding the responsibilities of a board and its role within the organization's life, nothing trumps overseeing the steady operation of the mission. This requires the board members:

- Know the mission.
- Understand the mission.
- Know how to measure the progress on implementing the mission, which includes knowing what metrics are being used. (I call this "knowing the score.")
- Represent the organization's mission to the community.
- Steadily provide and manage the resources needed to support the health and impact of the organization.

While overseeing the progress of the paramount role of a board, it still amazes me how little time some boards devote to ensure that the organization is executing its mission. The entire next section of this book will focus primarily on that particular core competency.

Agreements

No matter how close and unified a board is, challenges can cause friction and disagreements. Wise leaders plan for such occasions.

I once pastored a church where the opportunity presented itself to sell the property and buildings we owned and to relocate. We were experiencing explosive growth and facing parking challenges. The prospect of adding a fourth worship gathering felt daunting.

There was potential for deep division within the board and, subsequently, within the congregation. When our church was young, the board made decisions based on a consensus vote. Crucial decisions by the slimmest of margins were possible.

Two years before facing the possibility of selling our property and moving, the board had agreed that we would only proceed with complete unity and a unanimous vote on critical decisions. A simple majority vote could still pass less important decisions.

Let me emphasize that this process was not spelled out in our constitution or founding documents. It was an agreement we made before we faced a decision like the one about moving.

Faced with such a critical decision, I called for the congregation to participate in a three-day fast in seeking God's leading. We set before our congregation two choices: (1) stay or (2) sell and move. We began the fast on a Sunday evening and broke it by coming to the Lord's Table for Communion.

People shared what they had heard God say to them during their time of fasting.

Then we took a written vote. The votes were tabulated as the congregation continued to worship, and the results were announced before closing the gathering in prayer. The congregation had unanimously voted to stay and build. The board followed suit at its next meeting.

Sometimes deciding how you will arrive at a decision is more critical than your decisions.

That is true when it comes to other types of agreements. Critical issues are only sometimes spelled out in your founding documents. These include topics like:

- What authority lies with the board and what authority lies with the senior leader?
- How will the board express care for the senior leader?
- How does the board deal with unresolved relational conflict?
- How does the board communicate with the staff, the community, or the congregation?
- How does the board handle confidential communication?
- How does the board handle Human Resource issues?

Other issues are critical enough to consider how a board should approach them before they arise. These issues and other subjects are covered in Appendix B.

The Clearer, The Better

Unclear expectations cause people to refrain from engaging thoroughly. Some people will use their imagination and create their expectations.

Board members should refrain from using their imaginations when filling in the blanks around issues like their roles, responsibilities, and authority. They should be provided with clear guidance regarding each item and informed before they agree to serve their board term.

Some organizations do an excellent job of providing the clarity required before agreeing to serve on their board. The Boys and Girls Club of Oakland, California, is one organization that clearly defines its board members' job descriptions. It starts with their tagline, "Great futures start here!"

The way they approach expectational clarity blows the fog of confusion away. It starts with the board vision and includes a job summary, the term's length, and each member's primary responsibilities.

It concludes with six sections and how many annual hours are being asked to commit to each area, including:

- Meeting attendance (28 annual hours)
- Reading and responding (10 annual hours)
- Advocacy (20 annual hours)
- Guiding and planning (6 annual hours)
- Influencing (15 annual hours)
- Fundraising (21 annual hours)

They spell out board member expectations in a one-page format. The final statement at the bottom of the sheet summarizes the importance of the commitment. "The 100-hour year comes down to less than two hours per week in support of an organization that is making a vital difference in our community. The commitment we seek is modest, but it is time well spent."

When people join the Boys and Girls Clubs Oakland board, you can bet they know what is expected of them. If the board chairperson tells the newest member, "Run the next one out," she will not likely run to third base. Clarity has a way of getting everyone running in the same direction.

Boys & Girls Clubs of Oakland
"Great futures start here!"

Board Member Job Description

Board Vision: "We will develop a Board of Directors who have the necessary dedication, resources, and connections to meet our commitment to double our service to youth over the next five years."

TITLE: Director

JOB SUMMARY: Assists officers in overseeing the health and direction of the organization

TERM: Three Years

Primary Responsibilities:

- Attend board of directors meetings and participate in conference calls

- Attend any annual business meetings of the organization

- Participate actively in organizational strategic planning

- Vote on organizational policy and program issues

- Serve as a resource of knowledge and counsel to the executive office committees and other directors

- Assist in locating and developing funding sources for the organization
- Review and respond to all action and information requests from the executive office
- Serve as a liaison between the board of directors and committee chairs
- Represent the organization at the request of the chair
- Identify and nominate new board member prospects
- Make a generous personal contribution to support the work of the Clubs

NOTE: We ask for one hundred of the 8,760 hours that comprise a calendar year. If properly utilized, those one hundred hours can help save and enhance hundreds of children's and their families' lives.

The 100-hour year comes down to less than two hours per week in support of an organization making a vital difference in our community. The commitment we week is modest, but it is time well spent.

<table>
<tr><td>

Meeting attendance:

12 hours (at monthly board meetings)
3 hours (at the Salute to Youth Dinner)
5 hours (at the Golf Tournament)
2 hours (at the annual meeting)
6 hours at committee meetings)

</td><td>

Reading and Responding:

10 hours – Reading the Boys & Girls Club information and responding to that material, i.e., meeting notices, surveys, potential donor lists, etc.

</td></tr>
<tr><td>

Advocacy:

20 hours – Talking about Boys & Girls Clubs with family, friends, associates, business vendors, prospective vendors, religious groups, & civic organizations, etc.

</td><td>

Guiding and Planning:

6 hours – Attending and participating in the board retreat and a follow-up work session to the retreat.

</td></tr>
<tr><td>

Influencing:

15 hours – Convincing foundation trustees, local government officials, state legislators, business, and community leaders that Boys & Girls Clubs offer the "best bang for the buck" and are a wise investment.

</td><td>

Fundraising:

21 hours – They are placing calls, writing letters, and "making the ask" in support of the Boys & Girls Clubs. This time is best used in assisting with major fundraising events such as steak & burger dinners and the annual campaign.

</td></tr>
</table>

Section Three
Competency

Vibe Eclipse Model

Chapter 5
The Rhythm of Oversight

*Rhythm is something you either have or don't have,
but when you have it, you have it all over.*

- Elvis Presley.

Rhythm is the pulse of music.

- Ignacy Jan Paderewski.

I SPENT LAST NEW YEAR'S EVE and the first two weeks of this year in our local hospital in Bend, Oregon. We've got great medical care here. One of the features of St. Charles Hospital is that a patient is allowed to order room service. That's right; I could order anything I wanted for breakfast, lunch, and dinner anytime. If I got Jell-o, it would be because I ordered it. I didn't.

My sixteen-day hospital stay resulted from innocently slipping on an icy sidewalk at the bottom of our driveway. My problem was compounded because I landed on my right hip, which had been surgically replaced only thirteen months prior. The fall, one of sixty similar slips that morning in Bend, resulted in a fractured femur and a new hip replacement.

Happy New Year!

One of the things that stood out to me was how often someone came to check on my vital signs. The nurses were almost always cheerful, even a little too, when they checked my blood pressure, temperature, and heart functions in the middle of the night.

One's heartbeat and rhythms are critical to living a healthy life. The popularity of a song is also tied to its beat and rhythm. It also might explain why someone might love the Eagles while her son prefers listening to Prince and her granddaughter loves, loves, loves Taylor Swift. Give thanks for playlists and noise-canceling headphones. They have made family outings in cars far less acrimonious.

We've all almost certainly had one particular parent-child conversation. We likely had as a teenager with one of our parents, and if you have teens in your home, you've engaged in it again. It goes something like this:

Dad: Can you change the song on the stereo?

Teenage Son (TS): It's not a stereo dad. It's a sound system. It's playing my playlist, which is on random—

Dad: Just change it, okay?

TS: But Dad, this song is sic.

Dad: I agree. That's why I want you to change it.

TS: Not sick as in sick, but sic as in dope.

Dad: What? Never mind, change it. Why do you listen to that?

TS: I don't listen to the lyrics Dad. I just like the ________.
(I bet you can fill in the blank.)

I just like the *beat!*

The beat of a song makes us tap our shoes and nod our heads back and forth. It's the pulse... the heartbeat. Funny, while Junior enjoys the beat, it is the song's rhythm that makes him like it so much. It's easy to confuse beat with rhythm. They are not synonymous.

The Beat in the Boardroom (or Don't Step on Your Dance Partner's Toes!)

The beat of a song is its underlying pulse or the steady pattern of time; it's like a heartbeat. Rhythm is the intricate arrangement and patterns within the beat's framework. It gives the music its texture and groove.

In short, the beat is the pulse, the rhythm is the song's flow, and both are essential parts. The tempo of the song, i.e., its beat, remains constant throughout. In a nonprofit or a church congregation, the equivalent to the beat is its mission. While personnel or programs change, the mission remains consistent. It anchors the board and the team. What kind of heartbeat and rhythm do you find in your board of directors?

A chief responsibility of a board of directors is to keep the organization on its mission. Every other oversight responsibility and expectation exists to support that effort.

Sometimes, a wise person joins a board and suddenly, without explanation, he becomes highly arrhythmic. In other words, he can't keep a beat, and has lost all sense of rhythm. People unable to maintain the beat make lousy dancers. They don't make much better board members.

Boards and senior leaders that are in rhythm can create an atmosphere where people are served, lives are changed, and organizations thrive. Those boards should enter a Dancing with the Stars competition.

Before asking for that first dance with its senior leader, a board should be advised to avoid stepping on its dance partner's toes. In other words, a board must learn the difference between "overseeing" versus "overreach." Let me explain.

The Importance of Oversight

The word oversight has two contrasting meanings. The first definition is "an unintentional failure to notice or to do something." Some boards unwittingly and certainly unintentionally provided that kind of oversight.

Another meaning is "overseeing, supervising, or caring for something or someone." In some church congregations, the term elder is used rather than director or member. In the early church, board members were called elders, literally translated as "overseers."

Board members and officers are responsible for jointly overseeing the affairs and activities of the organization they represent, and acting together to hire the senior leader, create policies, watch over finances and assets, and make decisions regarding strategy and other essential matters.

No one is above being held accountable for their performance and behavior within the organization. That begins with the board chair and extends to the lowest person on the organization chart. Oversight is put into place because everyone needs to be accountable to someone. It is there to help good people from doing bad things. "Bad things" include making poor decisions, disregarding ethics, or legal requirements, ignoring the organization's financial health, or allowing destructive behaviors or poor performance to continue unabated.

Oversight can be tricky. It is easy for a board member to cross an invisible line and find himself in the "land of overreach." When a board provides healthy oversight, the senior leader and her team are supported and resourced to conduct the day-to-day activities that best serve their target audience and further the mission.

My good friend, Pastor Steve Willhite, shepherds a small church in the San Francisco Bay Area. The Refuge Church also operates a nonprofit organization on its bustling campus. Though the congregation numbers less than one hundred people, Steve and his board have discovered ways and means to provide space for a Head Start program. This ministry offers groceries and meals for under-resourced families (the church distributes tons of food every month) and a way to house the homeless during the wet, cold winters in the Bay Area. I often tell Steve that he should write a book about their accomplishments. The title would be *The Little Church That Could.*

From Oversight to Overreach

Some board members cannot help but get involved in the daily affairs of an organization. A board member, including the board chair, should never usurp the authority of the senior leader by going behind her back and speaking with other staff members about the organization's affairs. When this happens, staff and volunteer members cannot help but become confused about to whom they should report.

I was fortunate to work with Youth for Christ USA when I graduated from college. It was the first place I received excellent training. I was later trusted with significant local, regional, and national responsibilities. One legendary figure in YFC was Sam Wolgemuth. Sam was the first international president and later served as the board chairperson for YFC International. He also served as the board chair for World Relief. He wrote about the consequences of board members stepping beyond their roles and engaging in day-to-day operations. He warned, "Whenever a board member gets involved in the day-to-day operations of the organization he serves, he must be prepared to quit his day job."

In short, Wolgemuth pointed out a significant difference between oversight and overreach. Oversight, when provided by wise and vibrant board members, provides the organization with clear direction, support, and the needed resources required to do the work of the ministry. The same people strive to ensure that all legal obligations to maintain the organization's exempt status are fulfilled and that the organization has the appropriate policies, procedures, and strategies to allow everyone to perform at their best.

Overreach is equivalent to stepping on your senior leader's toes. It leads to confusion, loss of trust, and diminishing engagement. It is easier to oversee an organization when everyone is dancing to the same beat.

NOTE: There are seasons and life stages of a nonprofit or church. The board of directors will operate differently during each of those seasons.

For instance, in an organization's early stage, board members often jump into the day-to-day role that a staff person would fill. How does a board member help the fledgling nonprofit but not overreach as a board member?

Please refer to APPENDIX H for additional insights into this issue.

The Rhythm of Oversight:
Get Up and Dance to the Music

You know a song has a great beat and superb rhythm when you can dance to it. For over fifty years, people have been dancing to a particular song that emerged from a new genre of music in the 1960s. If jazz music were an actual family, there would be a few "crazy uncles" in it. One was the music style from the '60s scene in San Francisco was made popular by Jimi Hendrix and Sly and the Family Stone. It was known as psychedelic soul or just plain funk.

All we need is a drummer for people who only need a beat, yeah.

I'm gonna add a little guitar and make it easy to move your feet."

I'm gonna add some bottom so that the dancers just won't hide.

You might like to hear my organ, I said ride Sally, ride, ride.

Dance to the music, dance to the music, dance to the music...

\- LYRICS TO "DANCE TO THE MUSIC"

Our friend Greg Errico was the original drummer for the Family Stone. He confirms that the '60s music scene was as crazy as people say. Racial integration wasn't common then and Greg was one of the two white people in the band. His presence made the group stand out even more.

Here's the thing. Sly and the Family Stone played complicated music, but it was fun and easy to dance to. Their first hit was called "Dance to the Music." If it's unfamiliar, you can better understand what I mean if you Google and play it.

Cynthia Robinson is the first voice you hear, and she implores the listener to "Get up and dance to the music." Then you hear Greg come in with the drums. The beat is immediately discernable. Getting to Freddie Stone's guitar or Larry Graham's bass isn't required before you feel your feet tapping and your head nodding back and forth.

The song's lyrics are simple, and its beat is pronounced. The lyrics introduce many of the band members and the instruments by name. Freddie Stone (Sly's brother) begins by singing, "All we need is a drummer for people who only need a beat." The song is off and running with the band's rhythm section, each adding a part. First, the guitar, then what Larry Graham calls the "bottom" or bass, and Sly adds the keyboard (in this case, an organ). The mixture of the beat and rhythm is infectious.

"Dance to the Music" is not only a great dance tune, it also serves as a model for what I want to refer to as "the rhythm of oversight" of a board of directors. I want you to consider a board's oversight responsibility is similar to a music group's drums, guitar, bottom (bass), and keyboards (organ). A board can build its own great vibe by providing diligent and wise oversight of:

- The **Mission** of Drums is an organization's constant and unchanging beat. The board offers a steady hand in guiding the senior leader to focus on and maintain mission advancement.

- The Guitar of **Management**: This responsibility comes in two parts. Part One is ensuring that the organization is compliant and current with all federal and state requirements. Part Two is providing supervision, support, and resourcing one staff person who is the senior leader.

- The Bass of **Money**: The bass is called the "bottom," which is appropriate for overseeing a nonprofit's finances. But not only does the board carefully watch over the "bottom line," it also attends to managing its organization's assets and fundraising activities.

- The Keyboard of **Meetings & Messaging**: The board is responsible for overseeing its senior leader, its organization's assets and financial health, setting key policies, and making important decisions to help execute its mission. A healthy board meets to make decisions, create policies, oversee resources, and oversees strategy and then communicates to its staff, volunteers, donors, and organizational stakeholders with "one voice." Even when someone disagrees with a particular decision or direction, there is a unified commitment to execute it and harmony regarding how it is communicated to others.

The beat supplied by adherence to the mission is supported and enhanced by the rhythm of overseeing management, money, and messaging. Let's take a closer look at each one.

Mission

A board's metaphorical drum set focuses on laying the beat around the organization's mission. Board members serve their terms and depart. Senior leaders can come and go, as do financial supporters. Staff and volunteer turnover can be expected. Remember, rhythms are ever-changing, but the beat remains constant. The mission must have strong support and oversight from the board.

Do you have the right senior leader in place to ensure the focus and implementation of the mission? Is he supporting, equipping, developing, and deploying his paid staff and volunteers with excellence? Is the mission adequately funded? Are there enough finances to launch new initiatives? Are the donors being cared for and paid attention to? Are they kept up to date about what is happening in the organization? Does the board do a good job communicating its support of the senior leader to the donors, staff, and volunteers?

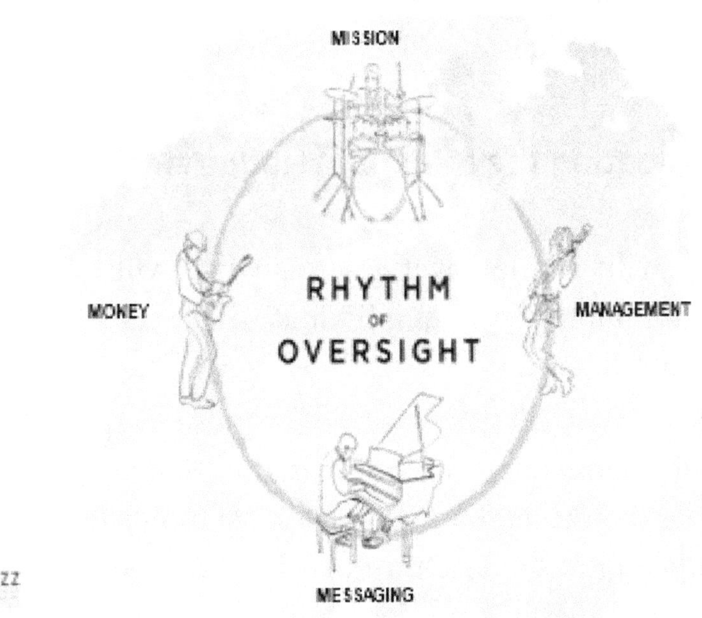

Management

There are two responsibilities to oversee when it comes to providing management oversight. The first one is that the organization remains in compliance and up to date with all of the state and federal government requirements pertaining to its nonprofit standing. The board may assign some of these tasks to staff members, committees, or individual board members, but the board is still responsible for the issues being addressed and correctly administered.

The second management responsibility is to oversee the senior leader. Although this is the primary management responsibility of the board, I will address it after reviewing the other requirements a board faces.

Meeting the Minimum Requirements

Let's start with a brief overview of what I will refer to as "meeting the minimum requirements." (Please see Appendix C for further details.)

FIDUCIARY DUTIES: I covered these responsibilities in the last chapter and am emphasizing them again at the risk of sounding redundant (too late). My point is that most people who serve on a board don't have the duties of care, loyalty, and obedience described to them. But, and here's the problem, every person who volunteers to serve on a nonprofit or church board is held legally responsible for fulfilling these responsibilities.

This is an excellent place to bring up the wisdom of having Directors and Officers Insurance (commonly referred to as D & O Insurance). This coverage is designed to protect individuals who serve on nonprofit boards from the possibility of a lawsuit. There are several reasons a nonprofit can be sued, including but not limited to lawsuits from people served by the organization, personal injury, employees (i.e., unlawful termination, etc.), vendors, creditor claims, reporting errors, etc. The organization can be held liable, but the board members are not personally responsible if the organization is adequately insured.

If a board member or the entire board should break the law, D & O insurance will not protect them from financial consequences. Most D & O insurance is a reasonable and wise expense for any nonprofit organization. If you don't have it, contact your insurance agent immediately and become educated on the type of coverage you should have. Then, get it!

LEGAL OVERSIGHT: One of the board's most critical roles is overseeing the organization's legal responsibilities. Appendix C covers this more thoroughly, but I will mention a few essential items here. The board must ensure the organization stays current with its state and federal filings. Were you aware that nonprofit does not necessarily mean tax-exempt? Do you know what kind of nonprofit you are? There are various categories, and they can have different legal and tax regulations and laws governing them.

It is important to remain knowledgeable regarding the founding documents. In those documents, the organization's mission and purpose were declared. The organization's responsibility is to stay focused on achieving those objectives.

Should the organization change its purpose or mission, it must update its documents and, if required, report those changes to the state where it is incorporated.

The board also oversees policies and procedures governing the organization, including:

- Conflict of interest policy
- Compensation policies for key employees
- Travel and reimbursement policies

Regarding legal oversight, the buck stops at the board level. A board of directors cannot say, "The buck never got here." You cannot overpay key employees. You cannot overextend lobbying for political issues or try and use your organization to sway political influence. Can you pass the public support test? In reality, a nonprofit belongs to the public and is for the public's good. The board is responsible for knowing and complying with the specific state and federal laws and requirements for the nonprofit and its particular organization.

DELEGATION: No one owns a nonprofit. It is one thing for a board to defer to the executive board, the board chairperson, or the senior leader in making a recommendation regarding a decision or direction – perhaps even to its founder from time to time. Even if a subgroup or individual carries much influence over decisions a board makes, none of the above parties has the same authority and the governing responsibilities relegated to the board as a whole.

A board can delegate authority to an individual or group, but it cannot delegate its responsibility to govern the organization. The board is responsible for the overall health and the nonprofit's performance.

This makes it essential to beware of a charismatic leader who desires to dictate the organization's direction. Look out for the individual or subgroups wishing to grab what they perceive as positional power or to assign an assumptive level of authority he or they believes comes with the role. Whenever necessary, refer to your founding documents to clarify what positions hold what authority. Usually, the board as a whole has the final say in leading the organization. The executive board should not act as a mini version of the board.

BOARD BASICS: Finally, a board has several other responsibilities that, if ignored, can become problematic. It must carefully identify, vet, and select new members. Too often, recruits are chosen for the wrong reasons. Therefore, a new member should be more qualified than a friend or family member, a business associate, or only because he is wealthy or has influence in the community.

When new board members begin their terms, they should be afforded an onboarding and orientation process. They should be welcomed and allowed to get to know the other members they will be serving with. In addition, the roles, responsibilities, and expectations should be carefully covered. No orientation is complete without covering the history and mission of the organization.

One of the most basic responsibilities of the board is to document decisions made by the board. When appropriate, the deliberation of those decisions and actions should be captured in the meeting notes and recorded.

Most board meetings reserve time to hear updates from the senior leader, other staff members, and committee heads. Prudent board members pay careful attention to these reports; if necessary, they validate what was shared if they feel something is amiss about the written report.

Overseeing the Senior Leader:

Sam Wolgemuth once said, "The board must understand that it has just one employee that it oversees, the CEO (i.e., executive director, lead pastor, senior leader, etc.), and the board needs to care for that employee as it expects him to direct and care for his staff."

The second management responsibility is to oversee the senior leader. All other staff positions report to the senior leader. Any deviance from this is likely to produce sore toes and sour notes.

It is important to note that the senior leader is accountable to the entire board. While he may have a close relationship with the chairperson, the senior leader is not accountable to the chair alone. Nor is he accountable to any other individual member of the board.

It is invaluable for the senior leader and board chair to share a relationship of mutual respect, deep trust, and keen collaboration. They share the same mission, goals, and objectives for the organization. Their ability to forge a close partnership is vital to the organization's success.

I know there are organizations where the senior leader serves as the board chair. That places much authority on one individual and can create a culture where the rest of the board carries around the authority that is equivalent of a rubber stamp.

Providing the senior leader with a careful balance of support and accountability includes providing her with candid feedback, making sure that she and her family are cared for. An annual review should be conducted (along with regular feedback and coaching sessions), and the board must make decisions allowing the senior leader to perform at the highest level possible.

Money

Key oversight responsibility for any board is maintaining financial accountability for the organization. Boards often serve as the organization's trustees, and in this way, they serve as stewards of its resources and always act on behalf of the organization's good.

Few board members will possess the financial acumen of Warren Buffet or Melinda Gates. Still, every board member must be willing to understand essential finances, read the financial statements provided, and recognize the danger signs that require proper management oversight to address and maintain the organization's financial health.

Looking back at the job description for the Boys and Girls Clubs of Oakland board members, it lists as a primary responsibility to "make a generous personal contribution to support the work of the clubs." In addition, each board is expected to contribute 21 hours of "placing calls, writing letters, and making the 'ask' to support the Boys and Girls clubs."

Some boards share different fundraising responsibilities. Still, it is imperative to be clear about what is expected of each board member when it comes to raising funds and what level of personal financial contribution is expected from each member.

Meetings and Messaging

Boards meet to make decisions, create new or revise old policies, or adopt new strategies. They are generally under tight schedules because their high-capacity members still have demanding day jobs! Once a board takes action, it becomes essential to communicate with the organization's key stakeholders. The message must be congruent when communicating to the community, staff, volunteers, and donors. Votes that pass by the slimmest of margins must still be presented as a decision adopted by the board. Carrying on disparaging conversations outside of the boardroom cannot be tolerated.

Healthy boards function as a single entity, therefore, they speak with "one voice." The One Voice principle refers to the practice that a board communicates the decisions made and directions taken in a spirit of unity and harmony. Even if decisions are passed by a hair's breadth, they are shared as coming from the entire board.

Should a board member feel the need to express disagreement, especially with others not on the board, it may be a sign of a more significant problem than simply one decision.

Create a Healthy Rhythm

These four oversight responsibilities must be performed like a quartet of musical instruments. There is a rhythm in how all the instruments function together. It is not always in the same order of how they are "played," but like the drums, the lead guitar, the bass, and the keyboards, when competent musicians play them, they result in sweet music.

Fifteen years after Jamie Davis debuted his album at the Palace of Fine Arts in San Francisco, Jody and I were invited to Hollywood to observe the Basie Band recording an album with legendary blues artists. All of our favorite people were there. Sam Beler was the executive producer, Scotty Barnhart directed the project and the band, Jamie sang, and Greg Errico flew in from Italy to participate in the event.

We also made new friends, including Carmen Bradford, Bobby Rush, and Lauren Mitchell. We had to leave early for a client engagement in the Bay Area, so we missed Robert Cray, George Benson, and Ledisi.

One of the most delightful people we got to know was Castro Coleman, known as "Mr. Sipp." Castro is an electrifying guitarist who sounds like B.B. King. Jody made that observation to Coleman as he rehearsed his first song. As it turns out, Mr. Sipp was mentored by the legendary "King of the Blues."

When we had the opportunity to speak with him later, Castro told us how excited he was to be invited by Scotty to play on the album. He said, "I've had the chance to play with a small horn section, but not the size and caliber of the Basie

Band." When the fourteen saxes, trombones, and trumpets hit their first notes on his song, Castro's bulging eyes said it all!

His guitar, a piano player, a stand-up bass, and a drummer set the beat and rhythm for the song. They were comping (accompanying) the horns that came in with the melody. They brought out the best in each other.

That is how a board of directors and a nonprofit's leadership should play together. When they do, the result is an excellent performance highlighted by masterful oversight that doesn't overreach. So what are you waiting for? Let me be your Cynthia Robinson and urge you to, "Get up and dance to the music!"

Oversight One
Mission

Chapter 6
The Oversight of Mission

Marry your mission, date your methods.

- Attributed to Andy Stanley and Craig Groeschel

"WE'RE ON A MISSION from God," is an iconic quotation from the comedy movie, *The Blues Brothers.*

Even today, when helping nonprofits and congregations develop their mission direction, someone almost always utters the phrase saying while creating their strategic plan.

If you watch the movie, you'll recognize that Jake and Elwood didn't really have a mission, not in the way mission is supposed to be defined. They had a short-term goal. When I think of examples of great mission statements, I think of some of the early ones from iconic American companies:

- Apple's initial mission was "To make tools for the mind that advance humankind."

- Google's mission: "To organize all the data in the world and make it accessible for everyone in useful ways."

- Amazon's mission: "To be earth's most customer-centric company, where people can come to find and discover anything they might want to buy online."

Those three companies have, by and large, stayed true to each of their initial causes. Having a clear mission that defines the activities of an organization is a huge difference-maker for the people working there. It is at least as necessary, if not more so, in a nonprofit organization.

Jesus Was a Missionalmaniac!

No one understood the need to be clear about one's mission better than Jesus of Nazareth. He announced his mission at the very onset of his ministry. Listen to his words in his hometown synagogue, "The Spirit of the Lord is on me because he has anointed me to proclaim good news to the poor. He has sent me to proclaim freedom for the prisoners and recovery of sight for the blind, to set the oppressed free and proclaim the year of the Lord's favor."

Roughly three years later, just before ascending into heaven, Jesus commissioned his Apostles with the same mission. Between the launch of his earthly mission and his Great Commission to the Apostles, Jesus sent the Twelve out in pairs (and then the Seventy in pairs) to perform the same activities he had done.

The mission is all about what people and organizations do. Whether it is Apple designing new technologies, Google organizing data, or a church like New Life Christian Center in Turlock, California, that describes its mission as "Loving people one step closer to Jesus." Verbs are the language of mission.

The best missions are significant causes.

Jesus sent his Apostles with a clear direction, "Go and make disciples." Furthermore, Jesus gave them a simple strategy. First, start in Jerusalem. Second, go into all of Judea and Samaria. Finally, extend the movement into all the world. It sounds like something Buzz Lightyear might say.

The Apostles went. The earliest churches did not have any buildings. They did not have a budget. They did not have a single professional clergy member. Yet, half of the Roman Empire followed the Galilean rabbi roughly three centuries later.

It did not stop there. The followers of Jesus kept going. Today, they continue to pursue making disciples. My two sons, Colin and Cameron, and a daughter-in-law Jess have been to India, Cambodia, New Zealand, Kenya, Nepal, Ireland, and South Africa. Colin, Jess, and our two grandchildren, Finleigh and Rowan, serve on the Youth with a Mission (YWAM) staff at the Harpenden Base, just outside London, England. Finleigh and Rowan have more stamps on their passports than I do on mine! YWAM knows about sending people, having deployed more than four million short-term missionaries in its sixty-plus-year history.

My point is simple, Jesus has (not "had") a compelling mission that is simple to understand and join. Does your organization possess a clearly defined and easily understood mission? Allow me to interrupt your reading and provide you with an easy and real-life exercise to do right now to do your organizational assessment. Do not read on without completing it:

Clarity Exercise Part One:
Purpose, Vision, and Mission Exercise

NOTE: Without looking at your organization's website, founding documents, or any collateral pieces, please fill out the exercise below:

1 Name of the Organization ______________________________

____

2 Your tenure on the board: [ ] Consider joining [ ] New member [ ] Less than one year   [ ] 1-3 years [ ] More than three years

3 What is the purpose of your organization? ___________________

____

____

4 Rate how effective the organization is in fulfilling its purpose: [ ] It is failing [ ] Poorly [ ] Fair [ ] Good but can improve [ ] Great!

5 What is the vision of your organization? ___________________

____

____

6 Rate the progress that the organization is making towards achieving its vision:
[ ] It is failing [ ] Poor [ ] Fair [ ] Good but can improve [ ] Great!

7 What is the mission of your organization? ___________________

____

____

8 What metrics do you use to gauge your progress towards advancing the mission?

____

____

____

9 Rate how well the organization is implementing its mission: [ ] It is failing [ ] Poor [ ] Fair [ ] Good but can improve [ ] Great!

10 How often does your board review the metrics and discuss the progress or lack thereof the organization is making toward advancing its mission?
[ ] Never [ ] Rarely [ ] At every meeting

Did you skip the exercise? If you did, please go back, and complete it. It will reveal gaps regarding being clear about the purpose, vision, and mission of the organization you serve.

Now, review your answers and record any pertinent insights, observations you have gained, or questions arising from the exercise.

<table>
<tr><td colspan="1" align="center">Clarity Exercise Part Two:
Personal Insights, Observations, Questions</td></tr>
<tr><td>Insights

</td></tr>
<tr><td>Observations

</td></tr>
<tr><td>Questions

</td></tr>
</table>

I encourage you to use this exercise with your senior leader and the entire board. It will provide you with a significant opportunity to determine how well-aligned your board is regarding these critical issues. You will be able to discuss and explore openly any existing gaps when it comes to the direction of where the organization is headed. This will allow you to get everyone "playing the same song" the way you intend it to be played.

My focus throughout this book is primarily on assisting a board to know, understand, and provide oversight for the advancement of its organization's mission. I intentionally spend less time focused on purpose and vision. The mission requires consistently reviewing whether the correct actions and activities are being performed. If the mission is not implemented, the purpose will never be fulfilled, and the vision will go unachieved. The mission is something you must do.

Talking is Not the Same as Doing

Conversations can lead to actions being taken. Let's be honest; they don't always. That is why vibrant boards maintain the rhythm gleaned from a superior combination of clarity, competency, and chemistry. It is essential to keep an eye on all three simultaneously. The best example of this is not Apple, Google, or Amazon. It comes from a carpenter from Nazareth who, nearly two centuries later, is still calling people to follow him!

When one reads the four gospels, it is impossible to miss Jesus living out his mission. He was on a mission, preparing others to follow him and to continue doing what he had done.

Many church congregations and faith-based nonprofit organizations claim they exist to fulfill the Great Commission. For example, the late Bill Bright founded Campus Crusade for Christ in 1951 and announced his vision to reach every nation group by the start of the 21st century. Cru (now its official name) has maintained its solid evangelistic focus for over seven decades.

Claiming the Great Commission as your organization's mission is one thing. It is entirely something else to live it out. Jody and I were invited to spend two days with over sixty full-time staff members at a megachurch. We were asked to facilitate workshops and discussions around building a healthy church culture.

The first day was full of learning and laughter. Talking about healthy relational interaction is always easier than engaging in it. We came to the second day when it was time to apply some of the communication skills we had covered. I decided to "set the ball up on the tee" and talk about a subject I knew the staff was well trained in. The congregation's mission was "to make disciples of all nations." It was displayed prominently in a beautiful work of art in the worship center's lobby. It was on every Sunday morning program they handed out. It was prominent on their website. The senior pastor had written a book on the subject, required reading for every staff and board member.

It was a safe subject to use while trying out the newly introduced communication methodologies we had just taught. This is where I should warn you, "Do not attempt this exercise at home."

I divided the room into eleven different ministry teams that were present at the offsite. I instructed each group team to discuss the following questions:

- How would each team define disciple-making?
- How did each team approach discipling people
  in each of their departments?

- What were each department's goals regarding disciple-making over the next twelve months?

Each group had forty-five minutes for the exercise. Each person was encouraged to share his or her viewpoints and opinions while remaining open to the perspective of others. They were to engage in spirited debate without becoming defensive or protective when others challenged their ideas. The exercise was to help them develop a culture where team members were more concerned about participating in a collaborative exchange focused on producing the best outcomes rather than defending their ideas.

When the discussions ended, the group regathered, and representatives shared how their teams answered the three questions. They began by defining "disciple-making."

What I thought would be a safe, teed-up conversation turned out to have far less common ground than I imagined. Only a few groups could remember how the lead pastor defined disciple-making. Fewer still had a plan for making disciples, and none of the teams possessed goals for the upcoming year. I had anticipated variations, but I fully expected that most of the groups would have remembered what the pastor had spent his thirty-plus years of ministry faithfully teaching and training his leadership about the subject.

The wheels started coming off the discussion, and I could tell by the look on the pastor's face that he was both deeply disappointed and embarrassed. In truth, many organizations (especially churches) teach about disciple-making, but few have agreed upon approaches to making it happen.

To execute a mission (disciple-making is only one example), an organization must describe what actions to take, what the results will look like, and what metrics will be used to inform its progress.

I often have church congregations telling me their mission is to be a part of fulfilling the Great Commission. I suggest they review two documents to determine whether they are dedicated to a disciple-making mission. They try to convince me that their mission is communicated in their constitution and various collateral pieces.

However, the documents I refer to are a calendar and a checkbook. Your founding documents can claim a particular mission. Your actual mission is where you spend your time and money.

What's the Score?

The missional scoreboard is one of the most critical items a board can review regularly. Let's imagine you and a friend are meeting at a baseball game. Your arrival is delayed, and the game is in the fourth inning when you get there. Glancing up at the scoreboard, you can see it is not working. You will likely ask your friend, "What's the score?"

Pretend your friend answers, "They've got four hits, and our team only has one. They hit a home run, but we haven't hit any. On top of all that, they've stolen two bases, but we haven't swiped any."

What would your next question be?

I bet it will be, "What's the score?"

Then imagine he tells you, "We're up two to one."

Activities like hits, home runs, and stolen bases can lead to scoring runs. But not always. The bottom line in winning a baseball game is outscoring the other team.

Let us apply the concept to a mission like making disciples. How does a congregation or an organization measure the effectiveness of the job they are doing? Some churches use the A, B, and C metrics method. It stands for "measuring attendance, buildings, and cash." But do those metrics quantify how well an organization successfully reaches people far from God and helps them become followers of Jesus? Do tracking attendance, offerings, and property development tell the story?

Scoreboards are essential, but only if they keep track of the metrics that matter.

Remember the story of the "Little Church That Could?" If you were to count the Sunday morning congregants or their offerings, you would likely conclude they were failing. You would be wrong! The Church is a beautiful example of a congregation understanding its target audience and mission.

Bigger has nothing to do with better. Attendance does not indicate that attendees are necessarily new disciples. A lot of church "growth" is more about congregational "transfer" than new people deciding to follow Jesus.

Scoreboards are Never More Important than When They are Missing

Do you ever notice that sports teams rarely keep score in practice? Unless you are scrimmaging, no one keeps score. But when a game is played, a nonfunctional scoreboard is a problem for the coaches, players, and those in the stands.

An example occurred shortly after Hurricane Katrina ransacked the southeastern United States in late August 2005. The Class 4 hurricane took over 1,800 lives and was the costliest natural disaster in our nation's history. New Orleans is still trying to rebuild over fifteen years later.

People are resilient, and once schools began to reopen, families tried to return to some form of routine. In southern American states, like Louisiana, "normal" involves high school football. Southern high school football takes a backseat to no other activity for sheer bedlam.

So, when one of the first high school championship games was held in New Orleans post-Katrina, it surprised no one when a standing-room-only crowd showed up to root for their school of choice. The rival marching bands competed to see which could be the most intimidating.

The first half was full of drama and excitement. The crowd cheered boisterously, and the score flipped in favor of one team and the other. But then something happened midway through the third quarter that confounded anyone paying attention.

Most people in the stands were no longer paying close attention to the game. Cheering noticeably subsided. Many people paid more immediate attention to their cell phones than to the game.

What happened?

People lost track of the score. The scoreboard had been destroyed by Katrina and had yet to be replaced. As people lost track of the score, they lost interest in the athletic contest even though it was for the high school championship.

A recent study showed that team members working on a project together are more likely to be motivated when reminded of their progress toward achieving their goals. Nothing is more invigorating than regular updates.

What does that have to do with a board of directors? I have served on a few boards that could succinctly tell anyone what the score was when measuring the execution of their organization's mission. My point is simple: too many board meetings lead to frustration, fatigue, failure, guilt, and especially boredom because directors have lost sight of the score and the game itself.

Keeping Score in the Book of Acts

Before Jesus ascended into heaven, he introduced a strategy for disciple-making to the eleven remaining Apostles. He raised it in the form of a commandment. Disciple-making was to: (1) begin in Jerusalem, (2) progress to all of Judea and Samaria, (3) and spread globally (see Acts 1:6). The remainder of Luke's writing details the growth of the Jesus Movement, its multiethnic and multicultural impact (Jews, Samaritans, and Gentiles), its geographical spread (mentioning specific cities and regional impact), and finally, its arrival and influence on the capital of the Roman Empire.

In the Book of Acts, Luke captured the early church's progress in obeying Jesus' command to "make disciples of all nations."

Baptisms performed

"Those that accepted his (Peter's) message were baptized, and about three thousand were added to their number that day." (This is but one passage of many reporting baptisms.)

Salvations recorded "And the Lord added to their number daily those who were being saved." (Frequency, every day in Acts 2:47.)

New leaders developed

A growing church identifies, develops, empowers, and deploys new leaders. Luke recorded new leaders that joined the original Jesus Movement, including Barnabas, Stephen, Paul (formerly known as Saul), Cornelius (and "all of his household"), Silas, Timothy, Priscilla and Aquila, Apollos, Dorcus, Lydia, as well as the recipient of the letter, Theophilus.

People group reached / Cities and regions where churches were planted

"This went on for two years so that the Jews and Greeks who lived in the province of Asia heard the word of the Lord... In this way the word of the Lord spread widely and grew in power." (The movement spread throughout all of Asia, increasing in influence in Acts 19:10, 20.)

"...those who lived in Lydda to Sharon saw him (Peter) and turned to the Lord... (Peter) in Joppa and many believed in the Lord." (Cities where the Gospel spread and the impact it was having in Acts 9.)

"The word of the Lord spread through the whole region..." (Geographical advancement in Acts 13:49.)"For the whole years, Paul stayed (in Rome) in his own rented house and welcomed all who came to see him. He proclaimed the kingdom of God and taught about the Lord Jesus Christ – with all boldness and without hindrance. (The Gospel reached the heart of the Roman Empire in Paul's lifetime in Acts 28:30, 31.)

When it comes to an organization's mission, it is critically essential to possess the following:

1. Metrics that are agreed upon and in place.
2. Metrics that are consistently tracked and up to date.
3. A plan to update all staff and volunteers on the organization's performance regarding its stated mission.

The Scoreboard in the Boardroom

First, the mission defines what activities should be focused on and the key outcomes to expect. Second, those actions and activities will bring clarity to the kind of senior leader that will be needed to lead the organization. Third, those same actions and activities will inform the organization of the required competencies of staff members and volunteers. That will clarify the kind of training and development required.

Finally, they will educate the organization's leadership on the necessary resources, including financial support, to achieve the strategic plans adopted by the board and senior staff.

It all starts with the mission.

As I conclude this chapter, let me tell you a story about the professional basketball team, the Golden State Warriors. Under their former ownership, their marketing tagline was, "It's a Great Time Out!" It was meant to encourage families to come out and enjoy a professional basketball game, devoid of the expectation of watching the Warriors compete for a professional basketball championship. I do not know who produced the marketing campaign, but I credit them for selling the experience, not the team's capability.

That era of Warriors seems like it was in BC times (Before Championships, that is). As I write this chapter, the Dubs recently defeated the Boston Celtics for their fourth title in eight years. Unless you are from the Bay Area, you will not remember the "It's a great time out" Warriors. They are now known for creating an iconic, revolutionary brand of basketball.

These same Warriors are not known for their mission statement. That is right; the Golden State Warriors have a mission statement. It does not mention titles or dominance and nearly fails to mention basketball.

A few years ago, I was invited to attend an event at San Quentin State Prison, located north of San Francisco in Marin County. It was hosted by Earl Smith, known as the "Death Row Chaplin." Besides the time he spent serving the inmates at San Quentin, Earl has also been the chaplain of the San Francisco 49ers and the Golden State

Warriors. At that particular event, two members of the Warriors attended, one being their general manager, Bob Myers.

When the event concluded, I spoke casually with Myers, a Bay Area native who played varsity basketball at San Ramon High School. Bob was warm and friendly, and I got to know some of the team's work at San Quentin included pickup games between Warriors' players and the inmates.

My experience led me to research my childhood favorite basketball team, and I eventually Googled their mission statement. Imagine my surprise when this is what I discovered:

> Our mission is to strengthen and empower underserved communities by providing programs and activities that promote self-esteem, respect, integrity, teamwork, and literacy.

Now that is a mission statement any nonprofit organization could be proud to own. The team goes on to say:

> The Warriors are committed to taking an active interest in the well-being of our community and to being great corporate citizens. We strive to develop life-long fans of the game of basketball through cause marketing programs and initiatives. We are dedicated to improving the quality of life for those who are underserved in our community.

After reading the statement, I was bursting with the pride of being a Dub fan! Their mission statement and how they live it out is even better than the recent championships they've won.

When I did not think a Stephen Curry led team could impress me more than they have in recent years, I came across the scoreboard they used to track their mission success. It differs from the scoreboard hanging from the Chase Arena's center court, where they compete. It is the one they use to measure how they are living out their mission. Here are the metrics they use and how they are doing:

- Community Events   320
- Students Served   2,263
- Minutes Tutored   3,128,140
- Math Problems Solved   9,200,000
- Physical Activity   20,528,850 Minutes
- Tickets Donated   15,000
- Wishes Granted   120
- Community Service   3,800 Hours

Those are eight activities they measure to make progress in serving the under-resourced population in the Bay Area.

They do all this and *much more* through their Warriors Community Foundation, which Mrs. Nicole Lacob expertly leads. This incredible foundation has helped fund over $30 million of grants supporting educational equity in San Francisco and Alameda counties. Last count, it has refurbished ninety basketball courts around the Bay Area to provide safe and clean places for children to play. It is involved in education (especially literacy), health care, and creating broad partnerships with other companies and organizations to feed under-resourced children and families. For example, for every point the Warriors score in a season, the foundation and its partners donate 100 meals to support Bay Area families. Consequently, in every game where the team scores 100 points, families in need will receive 10,000 meals. That is what I call generosity. In the basketball season of 2022-2023, the Foundation helped supply 1,122,350 meals for Bay Area food banks. In addition, the Foundation reached 1,189,350 individuals through their Warriors' social responsibility programs.

This does not even consider what the players, coaches, and team executives do on their own initiative. Bob Myers' presence at San Quentin was one example of executing their mission.

Are you a Warriors fan yet? I want your supporters, staff team, people you serve, and the entire community to feel the same way about your organization or congregation.

A board of directors' number one oversight priority and responsibility is to set up the organization for massive success in furthering its mission. Whether it is solving math problems, housing homeless veterans, rescuing and restoring human trafficked victims, making disciples, or finishing a layup in a pickup game at San Quentin, the success of a nonprofit organization comes down to mission-focused progress.

The people your organization serves will be better off from it. Your organization will be better because of it.

One Final Assignment

Before going on to the next chapter, grab a pencil or pen and complete the following exercise designed to help you think through how your organization can measure, manage, and provide board oversight for advancing your mission.

Clarity Exercise Part Three: Mission Management

Write your organization's mission statement here:

What are three or more key metrics to gauge if you are making a positive impact on implementing your organizational mission? List them below:

1.

2.

3.

4,

5.

Please list insights, observations, or questions regarding your responses above:

Observations:

Insights:

Questions:

Chapter 7
Who Moved My Mission?

Good ideas with great execution are how you make magic.

- Larry Page

Anchored to the rock and geared to the times.

- Founding motto of the Youth for Christ Ministry

I HAVE A CONFESSION TO MAKE. I am addicted to all things new. New thoughts are fascinating. New books, especially those written by favorite authors, readily find their way into my library. New relationships are stimulating.

My favorite "new thing" is an idea. A new concept, whether mine or someone else's, is invigorating. Everything we take for granted was once an idea. Whether a Model T or a Tesla, a Wright brothers flight or a journey to Mars, or a Well Fargo stagecoach delivery to the Internet, things once unfathomable existed in someone's imagination before they materialized.

Old-school Athenians loved ideas as well. If we could go back to the first century and find our way to the Areopagus during the time of the Apostle Paul, we would likely stumble into an animated discussion around a new idea.

Nonprofit leaders and church pastors tend to be learners. They constantly search for the latest tool, trick, teachable truth, or technique to help them serve their organizations or congregations. When I was a young senior pastor and my team members heard I was attending a conference, they were concerned I would come back and replace my new idea with my newest one. Constant "idea displacement" makes it impossible to gain momentum.

Looking back, I can readily admit that was no way to lead an organization.

Pastor Rick Warren recently transitioned from his forty-plus years of pastoring Saddleback Church. Rick was known for his imagination and his innovative ideas. He is best known for his book A Purpose Driven Life. The book launched countless seven-week campaigns called *40 Days of Purpose* offered by thousands of churches, with millions of people attending.

A friend of mine once had the opportunity to speak with Pastor Warren. My friend told Warren he had run the campaign with his congregation and said he hadn't seen "much of a bump in attendance." When Rick said nothing, my friend added, "I don't get it. Why do you guys grow so much."

Rick Warren smiled and replied, "We don't offer it just once. We keep offering it." If I can loosely translate Rick's words, it's, "We don't just offer the latest idea. We stay focused on the mission at Saddleback."

I am not saying there isn't any room for new and innovative ministry at your congregation or nonprofit organization. But when trying new approaches, the critical question is, "Will this help us execute our mission or distract us from it?" This chapter encourages you to be Missionalmaniacs in your passion for implementing your organization's mission.

Stumbling Blocks to Missional Momentum

Constant change can be a significant disruption when it comes to mission. Among other things, change can prevent momentum from ever happening. There are several ways organizations can lose not only mission momentum but also their way. A board must provide intentional oversight to help its leadership to stay faithful to the cause. It is essential to avoid five common stumbling blocks destined to disrupt missional momentum.

Mission Neglect

The first impediment is *mission neglect*. Neglect means to "fail to care for properly." Neglect may ignore providing attention to someone or disregarding someone or something. In this case, it is to ignore the mission.

I do not think boards intentionally neglect to oversee the execution of the organization's mission. That is the irritating aspect of neglect. It is rarely intentional. Neglect is the by-product of losing sight of the scoreboard.

Remember the story of the high school championship game played in New Orleans post-Hurricane Katrina? The fans in attendance lost track of the score and interest in the game itself.

Charles Spurgeon once said, "If it's a mist in the pulpit, it's a fog in the pews." When it comes to organizational mission, if it is a "mist in the boardroom, it's a fog in the field of ministry." When a board fails to stay informed about how the organization performs its mission, it will likely lose momentum and stall.

Mission Disconnect

The second stumbling block is *mission disconnect*. When a board does not track its missional progress, it is difficult to determine whether its actions and activities have a meaningful impact.

The Refuge Church is about serving the marginalized and under-resourced people in their neighborhoods. But they do not just feed hungry people. Pastor Steve Willhite prioritizes his ministry team members to connect with their hungry neighbors, pray for them, and be ready to share the Good News with them when given the opportunity.

Pastor Steve understands that someone can pass into eternity with a full stomach but on an empty soul. He has ensured the Refuge's mission is connected to Jesus' Great Commission.

Consider the faith-based nonprofit or church congregation you serve. Is its mission in alignment and connection to the mission of Jesus? It is possible to do good in this world but disconnect the Good News from the good work.

I have had countless conversations with well-meaning pastors who tell me theirs is a teaching, worship-centered, or community-focused church. They often add, "But I'm not an evangelist." They have a built-in excuse for not focusing on connecting with people who are relationally distant from God.

Is your organizational mission connected to the mission of the One who said he "came to seek and to save that which is lost?" Suppose your organization's target audience is people who struggle with homelessness, addiction, incarceration, human trafficking, teenage pregnancy, or other challenges. Do you connect those people with the Good News of Jesus?

I get it when leaders tell me they do not have the gift of evangelism. I do not have the gift of service, but I need to serve. I do not have the gift of intercessory prayer, but I need to pray. If your organization needs to be more assertive on evangelism, it may mean you should partner with an organization or a congregation whose strength lies in that area.

Mission Drift

A third mission stumbling block is mission *drift*. The Pixar movie *Up!* featured Dug, the dog who was constantly distracted. No matter Dug's focus on something, he quickly cried out, "Squirrel!" and chased one should it scurry by him. It was funny in the movie. It is not when it comes to mission advancement.

Mission focus is often challenged by a variety of things scurrying by. Good causes are often the enemy of great missions. Good causes can be the new fascinating shiny object or bushy-tailed, distracting squirrel.

Organizations, like people, do not intentionally drift. I have never counseled a married couple who admitted they woke up one day and decided to drift away from each other. It is common for leaders to set out to accomplish an intended result within a given time frame but lose focus and switch priorities. People and organizations drift, and they do so slowly.

Were you aware that commercial air flights, even on autopilot, must constantly correct course? This is to adjust to the constant drift created by the surrounding conditions. If not for constant course corrections, cross-country flights would end up in places not intended on their passengers' itineraries. Organizations are like commercial flights.

When I was a freshman at the University of California, Berkeley, I received a phone call from a friend who asked me if I wanted to make a few dollars by refereeing a 4th – 6th grade flag football game at our local YMCA. One morning game became a five-and-a-half-year relationship and the opportunity to develop some raw leadership muscles.

The Young Men's Christian Association has its own mission drift story. The YMCA was founded over 175 years ago by George Williams. Williams started the organization to provide bible studies and prayer meetings as an alternative for young men lured into bars and brothels during the Industrial Revolution in downtown London.

The YMCA was an early example of a parachurch ministry that crossed England's strict lines of church denominations and social classes. It flourished early on and survived the Civil War and World Wars I and II.

"The Y" is also somewhat of a Who's Who in faith-based history. Dwight L. Moody started in Christian ministry with the YMCA, and professional baseball player turned evangelist Billy Sunday was one of the American YMCA leaders. Oswald Chambers wrote the classic, *My Utmost for His Highest*, and was a YMCA chaplain during World War I.

What happened to its commitment to the cause of Christ? As far as one can discern, nothing significant occurred. There was not a major scandal. There was not a well-publicized renouncement of beliefs. A slow, gradual, and unintentional drift occurred until aerobics classes replaced bible studies, and Y-membership was more about bodybuilding than character building.

Organizations stray. To avoid drifting requires an ongoing board oversight that willingly reviews the organization's faithfulness to its mission. Mission drift occurs when the printed mission statement, whether on a marquee sign, on a website, or in numerous collateral pieces, no longer resembles what happens in the day-to-day life of the ministry.

When an organization is allowed to continue drifting, confusion replaces clarity and gaps in the services provided. There can also be leadership gaps. When leadership gaps arise, people often step in to fill them. Guess what? They are not usually the most qualified, healthiest, or best person to be in those positions.

Multiplie Missions

A fourth stumbling block can emerge when mission drift continues: *multiple missions*. Greg McKeown authored the book *Essentialism*. He says, "The word priority came into the English language in the 1400s. It was singular. It meant the very first or prior thing. It stayed singular for the next five hundred years. Only in the 1900s did we pluralize the term and start discussing priorities. Illogically, we reasoned that by changing the word, we could bend reality. Somehow, we could now have multiple 'first' things."

I want you to think about the mission in the same way. When an organization believes it can have and maintain multiple missions, it divides its attention, resources, leadership, and impact into small, bite-sized bits. Everything suffers.

Years ago, while working on a goal-setting workshop, I coined the term *goalible*. It was meant to combine the word "goal" with "gullible." We become goalible whenever we believe we will achieve more things in life if we set more and more goals. The reality, however, is that each of those goals is competing for the same limited amount of time and resources. Instead of achieving more, we end up accomplishing less.

Studies have demonstrated that the more goals an organization has, the less likely it will achieve them. While presenting at the Global Leadership Summit, Franklin Covey's Chris McChesney referenced the diminishing return of setting too many goals. His findings were as follows:

Number of Goals	2-3	4-10	11-20
Goals Achieved with Excellence	2-3	1-2	0

If that is true for something like goals, imagine the law of diminishing returns when applied to multiple missions. So, a board of directors must ensure that the senior leader directs her staff and volunteers to advance the mission. The surest way is to have regular updates on the mission's scoreboard.

Mission Memory

A fifth and, at least for this list, final stumbling block to missional progress is *mission memory*. The easiest way to define this obstacle starts with the phrase, "We used to..." or "I remember when..."

Good times from past times are enhanced with time, while the challenges or painful failures are diminished. I recently had a conversation with a friend who had just completed a long transitional role at a church in the Bay Area. He told me, "My biggest challenge was that many of their board members had been a part of the congregation during their most impactful years of ministry. When they talk about the current state of the church, they want to believe that they are still that large, thriving ministry they once were.

My friend said the church reminded him of an aging athlete who had not stopped recently to look at himself carefully in the mirror.

Some churches that used the attractional ministry model years ago and have experienced a sharp decline yearly do not stop to realize they are no longer attractional. Memories not balanced with reality checks can be misleading; when board members and the senior leader track metrics measuring missional impact, the organization's current state stays focused.

Youth for Christ had a foundational motto they used in their early years. It continues to guide the organization since its inception in the 1940s. It is: "Anchored to the rock and geared to the times." It has served as a reminder that mission is more stable than methodology. Methods change. It is one of the reasons the Church has endured for nearly two thousand years. It has endured and advanced through its birth, early development, the Middle Ages, the Reformation, the Puritans, the Great Awakening, modernism, the Jesus Movement, and postmodernism. Last rites have been given to the Church on multiple occasions, yet it remains, and in some places, it flourishes and thrives.

The Church has given birth to parachurch ministries and nonprofit organizations, and it exists in sizes from two (as in "where two or more are gathered together in my name") to more than 100,000. Some congregations meet in multiple locations in multiple states and nations and multiple forms of gatherings.

Churches and nonprofit organizations can ride wild waves of growth and impact when they put their mission ahead of programs. Your organization may not be "mega" in size but can have a huge (as in a "little church that could") impact on the people it serves.

A board is in place to ensure the organization does not stumble over distractions or fumble its mission. Every nonprofit organization and church congregation deserves a board of directors comprised of vibrant people to ensure sustainability and advance its mission.

Oversight Two
Management

Chapter 8
The Oversight of Management...
The Senior Leader

The problem with the bottleneck is that it is always at the top of the bottle.

   - Peter Drucker.

The question, "Who ought to be the boss?" is like asking, "Who ought to be the tenor in the quartet?" The man who can sing tenor.

   - Henry Ford

WHAT IS THE IDEAL OUTCOME that should emerge after every board meeting? I am not talking about just some board meetings but every board meeting. Some possible answers include the following:

- The board should come away with clarity about the organization's financial status.

- Board members should leave the meeting with an update on the missional scoreboard. (Give yourself extra credit if you suggested it.)

- There should be updates on staff, ministry progress, and donor relations.

- There should be a status update on how the senior leader is doing personally and professionally.
- The board should hear at least one good story from a staff member or a volunteer who is inspiring and uplifting.
- The meeting should be drama-free and void of negative conflict.
- Most of the above.
- All of the above.

In short, the ideal outcome from any board gathering is about the people investing their lives in advancing the mission and meeting the needs of those the organization exists to benefit. The top benefactor of a good board meeting should be the senior leader and the entire ministry team.

This type of material should be taught in a Board 101 class. I have observed enough boards to know that some members want to get deep into the thick of day-to-day operations. An individual member who often has an opinion on what should be done and cannot wait to tell the senior leader or the board what to do can be problematic to organizational chemistry. I will remind you what Sam Wolgemuth said about a board member who gets deeply involved in the organization's day-to-day operations. Sam said, "He must be prepared to quit his day job."

While the primary oversight responsibility of the board is executing the organization's mission, the second is providing oversight to the organization's management. In an earlier chapter, I wrote that management oversight covers two parts.

The first one is what I refer to as "meeting the minimum requirements" of the organization's legal responsibilities. I refer you to APPENDIX C for greater clarification on what this entails.

Overseeing the Senior Leader

The remainder of this chapter will address what it means to oversee personnel management. I believe, in the case of a nonprofit or a church congregation, the board oversees only one person, the senior leader.

This is a crucial oversight responsibility for a board to handle, and when it is done well, everyone benefits. I am amazed by how often it is mishandled in churches and nonprofit organizations. I have seen some incredible partnerships forged by board chairs and senior leaders and between entire boards and leadership teams, resulting in outstanding ministry outcomes. I have personally been the recipient of beautiful partnerships with board chairs.

I have also witnessed some crazy consequences when it comes to power struggles. I recently heard of a story where the senior leader got into a vision disagreement with his board and fired every board member. It turns out his constitution granted him the authority to do so. Let that serve as a reminder to dust off your copy of your organization's constitution and refresh your memory about what it says.

The most bizarre power struggle I have ever experienced was the incident I briefly introduced earlier in this book. I am referring to the gathering in the church conference room with the elders on one side of the table, the deacons and deaconesses on the other, and the lonely pastor on the other. The elders had invited me to attend the meeting to see if I could help them resolve the conflict they were experiencing with their pastor.

I began the session by asking each person to tell me their perspective of what was causing the friction.

The elders' narrative began with a history lesson regarding the congregation's original by-laws, which allowed the lead pastor to be an ex officio, non-voting elder board member. Their former pastor fought hard to be recognized as a full member of the board. He took the elders and the congregation through a series of sermons and made his case for including a pastor as an elder. He twice failed to garner enough votes to change their constitution.

A third attempt to amend the by-laws was successful by the slimmest of margins, and he was installed as a board voting member.

The pastor had inadvertently convinced the congregation that a pastor should be a board member, not just the lead pastor. The other pastors on the staff were also installed as voting members of the church board.

The lead pastor and his lead associate constantly disagreed during board meetings. The associate felt unsafe having those conversations at staff meetings because the pastor shut him down. At board meetings, they were equals.

The lay elders were tired of the constant arguing and resigned from the board. When I met with them, the board consisted of a single lay board member (the chairperson), the new lead pastor, and his associates. The new lead pastor had been at the church for about a year.

It became apparent that the new pastor had not paid attention to the congregation's constitution. He was unaware who had the authority to hire and fire his staff. According to the by-laws, the board (not the lead pastor) held hiring and firing power. The new pastor did not find this out until he attempted to terminate one of his staff members to hire a new associate. The remaining two pastoral elders supported their colleagues and acted with the board's authority. They blocked the lead pastor from making the staff changes he wanted.

It was a lot to take in, and I did my best to keep up. I asked a clarifying question, "Do you all do staff evaluations?" They all nodded. So, I asked as I pointed to the three associate pastor elders, "Who does yours?"

"He does," they said, pointing to the lead pastor.

I looked at him and asked, "Who does your evaluation?"

'They do," he responded, meaning the rest of the board, including his three associates.

I thought, "And you all don't see an issue with that?"

I looked at the deacons and deaconesses sitting quietly on their side of the table. "What can you tell me about what I should know?" I asked them.

One man slowly raised his hand and quietly said, "No one mentioned why we're here. Someone should tell you about when the pastor called an emergency congregational meeting when nearly all the elders were out of town."

When he was sure he wasn't going to be interrupted, he continued. "Pastor asked congregational members to stay after church for an emergency meeting. The only subject on his agenda was to amend the constitution to allow only the senior pastor to serve on the elder board. If his motion passed, all other pastors would be removed from the board."

I glanced around the room to see if anyone wanted to correct or amend the story. No one did.

The deacon continued. "We had a quorum, but our by-laws call for two weeks to pass before a vote can be taken."

The board chair interrupted. "Then we got back in town." He said it with a bite.

The lead pastor interrupted. "The elders sent out a scathing letter to the congregation that defamed my character. Here's a copy of the letter," he said as he gave it to me. "This is a page-and-a-half character assassination."

There was a palpable sense of both anger and sadness in the room. No one wanted to be there.

The problem was years in the making, but the summary was delivered to me in less than sixty minutes. In addition, they had waited for over six months before they finally reached out for outside perspective and help.

Dr. Phil usually gets more time with his clients before he is asked to render advice. I had not even asked my first, "How's that working for you?" before the board chair asked, "How long should this take to fix?"

I wanted to scream, "This is a magic marker, people; it isn't a magic wand."

I smiled before saying, "I don't think you're asking for a solution yet. But if you insist I give you one, let us start by cutting the baby into thirds, and each group gets to keep one-third of the congregation."

"Like Solomon?" one of them asked.

"Exactly," I replied, "like Solomon."

This is an extreme case of board-senior leader dysfunction. It makes a strong case for clarifying where the ultimate authority lies within an organization.

Know Where the Authority Lies

An organization's founding documents ultimately clarify where the lines of authority and accountability are drawn. The chances are that most founding documents will declare the final authority will lie with the board of directors, and the day-to-day operational control will rest with the senior leader.

That means the board hires, supervises, oversees, and evaluates the senior leader's performance. In turn, the board empowers the senior leader to do the same with his staff.

Understanding where the authority rests is only one aspect of an organization's operations. Once everyone understands who is in charge, the bigger question becomes how the board of directors does; the board chair, the senior leader, and the staff work together to ensure everyone stays on point regarding mission execution.

Bring the Love

Before addressing "who does what?" I want to talk about three practices to help everyone work in healthy and effective ways. In short, the board, senior leader, and staff should bring the love, be honest, and sing harmoniously.

First, everyone must *bring the love.* The late Bill Campbell was affectionately known as "the Trillion Dollar Coach." He was a former college football coach turned businessperson who later became the coach of some of Silicon Valley's most famous business leaders. Bill coached the likes of people who were on the short list of Who's Who of Sand Hill Road, known for its concentration of high technology companies.

Campbell was famous for his personable but no-nonsense coaching style. He didn't put up with petty B.S. (not code for Bible Study). He was equally remembered for emphasizing that love has a valuable place in the corporate world, not a concept often spoken of in such a setting.

Many people who knew Bill best explain he was known for treating people exceptionally well and prioritizing the importance of relationships in business. People are often surprised whenever love finds its way into offices and conference rooms in corporate organizations.

I am always surprised when love is missing from faith-based organizations. I am incredibly disappointed when it is missing on the board level. It is critically important to prioritize the relational side of the board-senior leader interactions. Ask yourself the following questions:

- "Are we as a board up to date on how our senior leader and his staff team are doing personally?"
- "Do your board members know the names of the senior leader's spouse and children?"
- "Are your board members aware of any health issues that staff members or critical volunteers face?"
- "Do your board members appropriately know of any serious spiritual, financial, or relational challenges the key organization members face?"
- "Does your board pray for the senior leader, staff members, or volunteers?"

Board members cannot allow themselves to be so relationally disconnected that they are clueless about the personal goings-on in the organization. While board members feel the responsibility of the organization's financial health deeper than anyone else (except perhaps the senior leader), they must also have a feel for the relational health of the organization.

Having said all of this, let me add that the board is not responsible for creating the day-to-day culture of the organization. That responsibility falls directly on the senior leader and his team.

Disconnected relationships extract a penalty when operating at total capacity, achieving goals and objectives, and executing the mission. Board members are not expected to have intimate connections with every staff member or donor in the organization. Neither are they expected to remain aloof and distant. Relational connection is irreplaceable in a faith-based organization.

Are your board members in touch with God? How does the Holy Spirit speak to board members when faced with significant decisions or addressing the organization's needs? Who speaks for God during the board meetings? I am not asking who provides the opening devotional. Devotionals and opening prayers often are too much like the singing of the National Anthem before a game begins. Once the "amen" is said, it is time to "Play ball!" After the devotional, how often is God addressed during the meeting? Are his wisdom, direction, and discernment sought during the discussions?

It is critical for the board chair, the senior leader, and the board to stay in touch with each other and with God.

Be Honest

Second, *be honest with each other.* Paul admonished Jesus' followers to "speak the truth in love." It is easier said than done when a board meeting is often kept to ninety minutes or less. That does not leave much time for spirited discussions or respectful but passionate debates where members may speak truthfully about their respective viewpoints and opinions designed to shape strategy and decisions.

Honest give-and-take conversations give way to rubber-stamped decisions usually presented by the senior leader or the board chair. This decision-making methodology saves time in the short term, but the lack of diverse perspectives can prove costly in the long term.

Fostering spirited debates without allowing disagreements to become personal can be the surest way of developing healthy board culture. After all, the goal of a good board meeting is to resource the senior leader to lead the pursuit of the mission, not enjoy Kumbaya moments of bliss.

Sing in Harmony

There are a lot of rules vocalists must abide by when singing in harmony with one another. Voices should not overlap to preserve clarity in the vocal performance. The same rule applies to leading a nonprofit organization or a church congregation. Personalities in leadership positions, whether they sit on the board or serve in a vital leadership position, must not cross into each other's areas. It sounds more straightforward than it is.

Operating harmoniously between a board of directors and a senior leader is also a delicate process. But the results can be as wonderfully pleasant as listening to an acapella group like Pentatonix perform their version of the song "Hallelujah." It starts with recognizing who is the singing lead at any given time.

Start with the Senior Leader's Notes

The senior leader sings "lead" in the day-to-day operations of a nonprofit or a congregation. Her "musical score" will look something like this:

SENIOR LEADER'S JOB DESCRIPTION: Does one exist? If so, does it describe the responsibilities the position carries and what outcomes are expected from her? Does it provide freedom in how the senior leader can obtain those outcomes, or does it tell her how she is required to do her job? Please pay attention to the word *how*.

Some job descriptions document in detail how a leader is to run the organization. Often this results from one or several predecessors experiencing failure and making mistakes. Consequently, items to ensure how a senior leader does her work are added to the job descriptions until it becomes nothing other than a detailed To-Do checklist. It is best when a board can clearly describe what winning looks like for the organization and allow the senior leader the freedom to figure out how to achieve those results.

Review your organization's job description for the senior leader and make any adjustments to fit the outcomes you want to see that person achieve.

ACCOUNTABILITY: To whom is the senior leader accountable? She is answerable to the entire board. It gets clunky if the leader doesn't regularly meet with a liaison assigned by the board (generally the board chair) to address issues, problems, and needs with the senior leader.

The chair and the senior leader should meet regularly to stay current on the organization's progress, the challenges the senior leader is encountering, and how the senior leader is doing on a personal level.

MAKINGTHE CHAIRPERSON AND SENIOR LEADER RELATIONSHIP WORK: For the chair and senior leader partnership to work, four essential qualities must be present. First, they must *trust each other*. The strength or weakness of their trust will affect every other aspect of their relationship. Any absence in their harmony will make their performance sound like a duet between a flute and a tuba. When these two individuals leverage relational trust, everyone in the organization wins.

Second, their trust must be strong enough to *engage in disagreement, even when it leads to uncomfortable conflict.* One of my favorite proverbs is, "As iron sharpens iron, so one person sharpens another." When iron sharpens iron, sparks fly. Ron Knapp is a good friend of mine. He was the board chair of a church congregation when I served as the interim pastor. Ron and I did not always agree with each other. But instead of hindering our ability to partner together, our occasional friction enhanced it. We trusted the strength of our relationship to handle different viewpoints or perspectives. Even when they varied wildly, and each of us held strong opinions, we leaned into and not away from the disagreement. We did so to arrive at the best decision for the sake of the congregation. Sometimes, someone else on the board had a better idea than either of us. What I remember best about those exchanges was that Ron never put me in a position where I felt I had to defend my position. I hope I did the same for him.

Third, the two leaders must *mutually commit* to the organization's success. It is easy for personality conflicts to create a toxic culture on the board. It isn't uncommon for people to take sides. These kinds of disputes are like an airborne virus. When leaders are more committed to the organization's well-being than to winning petty arguments or getting their way, it is unlikely toxic behavior will take root on the board. One principle we like to encourage in organizations is something we got from Intel. It is a simple but powerful phrase: "Disagree and commit." It is fair to disagree and debate about a decision until it is made. Once made, however, it becomes essential to support the decision with total effort, even if someone is wholly opposed to it. Disagree and commit anyway. It is a great principle to make your own.

Finally, both leaders must do everything they can to *avoid power struggles.* One excellent strategy I have used with success over the years is concentrating on serving others and always acting in their best interests. Let me emphasize, this does not mean I necessarily acquiesce to the other person. Sometimes working in their best interests is respectfully disagreeing with their viewpoint. Vulnerability-based honesty covers a multitude of sins and avoids a multitude of needless power struggles.

In short, one of the best ways to oversee the senior leader of an organization is to equip her with a trusting, open, transparent, supporting, and challenging relationship with a liaison to the board, usually the chairperson.

AUTHORITY OF THE SENIOR LEADER: The senior leader must understand what authority she possesses and what she doesn't. What decisions is she dependent on the board to make, and what can she do without its approval?

For instance, once the budget is approved, is the senior leader free to make financial decisions on behalf of the organization as long as those actions do not exceed board-approved parameters? Are there limited amounts that, when exceeded, require special board approval? Is the senior leader free to change how money is spent, or is she bound only by what is in the budget?

Does the senior leader possess actual hiring and firing authority regarding staff oversight? Are any restrictions spelled out in the organization's by-laws restricting a senior leader from making staff decisions? This can be tricky in some churches that require congregational approval when hiring (calling) or firing particular pastoral positions.

The senior leader carries many responsibilities. It is only fair to her to be clear about what is expected of her, to whom she is accountable, and what kind of authority she has. One of the primary responsibilities of a board is the oversight of the senior leader in such a way that the senior leader's voice can be heard. The board sings background harmony to the senior leader's lead in day-to-day operations. Good backup singers never step on the lead singer's voice!

The Board Chairperson's Notes

The board provides the senior leader with the support, accountability, authority, resources, and oversight required to be successful. Once the senior leader steps into the boardroom, he acquiesces the lead singing role to the chairperson.

The chairperson's position is the most prominent and vital on a nonprofit board. He sets the tone for how well the organization is governed. That said, the chair position does not carry greater decision-making authority than any other role on the board. The chair does not have additional voting power. Yes, the chair may have influence, but influence is not the same as constitutionally given authority. When a chair begins to make independent decisions or speaks on behalf of the board without being empowered, he or she likely becomes the focal point of dysfunctional performance.

The senior leader and the board chairperson must figure out a way to work together for the sake of the entire organization. They must come to a place where they have clarity about the "song they are going to play and how they are going to play it."

When the board chair and the senior leader are not in harmony with one another, the discord cannot be hidden from others on the board and even within the organization. When the flute hits a wrong note, the audience may not notice, but when the tuba and the saxophone are playing the same song differently, it ruins the entire performance.

LEADS THE BOARD: While the board chair often serves as the liaison to the senior leader, his chief responsibilities lie in how he leads the board. He must remind the board members of their fiduciary and oversight roles, hold members accountable to meet/ fulfill the commitments they make individually and collectively, and come prepared for every meeting. In addition, he has the members responsible for representing the organization in their network of relationships and participating in fundraising that meets the board's commitment in that area.

MAINTAINS ORGANIZATIONAL ADHERENCE TO THE FOUNDING DOCUMENTS: A chairperson must possess an especially keen understanding of the founding documents and ensure the board complies with them. No exceptions. No compromises. Should other members want to look the other way, the board chair must insist they handle all decisions in a way that is faithful to what the documents say. For example, should the by-laws outline term limits for board tenure, the chair must uphold those limits, even if it means losing a strong, contributing, and influential person for a period of time.

HOLDS BOARD MEMBERS ACCOUNTABLE: In addition to understanding the organization's governing rules, the chair must be willing to hold every member accountable for their performance. A significant aspect of this will be ensuring members come prepared to engage in every meeting fully. When a board member comes unprepared because he hasn't reviewed last month's meeting notes or doesn't review the financial data and reports, it is like a musician coming into a recording session without becoming familiar with the music charts. To ensure the best meeting possible, the chairperson must be willing to call out members who repeatedly come to the meeting unprepared. Furthermore, board members are responsible for being punctual so meetings can start on time and stick to the allotted time frame. The chair should not wait for stragglers or late arrivals to begin the meeting. When there are repeat offenders, it is the chair's responsibility to have a corrective conversation.

SENIOR LEADER REVIEW: The chair is responsible for ensuring the senior leader has a formal review every year. The chair should perform the senior leader's review and include at least two other members when it takes place. Too often, a senior leader does not hear from his board how his performance is perceived. This can lead to poor habits being perpetuated or poor performance somehow being tolerated.

Worse yet, the uncomfortable conversation can be put off until the frustration grows to the point of dismissing the senior leader. When this happens, the senior leader is blindsided to learn his board had concerns about his performance for a long time before they decided it was going to terminate him. It isn't that no one had conversations about his performance. None of the talks were with him.

A board chairperson does not just draw up the agenda for the meetings. Neither does the chair usurp the authority given to the senior leader or start to dictate how the leader should do her job. A high-performing board chairperson makes sure the organization is governed correctly, holds the other board members accountable to fulfill their responsibilities, serves as the liaison to the senior, makes sure the leader has a yearly review, and keeps the board focused on the priority of advancing the cause of the organization.

The Board Member's Notes

I have already covered the general oversight responsibilities of the board in general. These are covered in the rhythm of oversight and include overseeing mission, management, money, and messaging.

This is an excellent place for a quick review of the job description of the Oakland Boys and Girls Club board members addressing more specific responsibilities. These responsibilities help board officers "oversee the health and direction of the organization" and include:

- Attending board of directors' meetings and participate in conference calls
- Attending any annual business meetings of the organization
- Participating actively in organizational strategic planning
- Voting on organizational policy and program issues
- Serving as a resource of knowledge and counsel to the executive office committees and other directors
- Assisting in locating and developing funding sources for the organization
- Reviewing and respond to all action and information requests from the executive office
- Serving as a liaison between the board of directors and committee chairs

- Representing the organization at the request of the chair

- Identifying and nominating new board member prospects

- Making a generous personal contribution to support the work of the organization.

The Boys and Girls Clubs of Oakland have thought through what efforts it takes to build and maintain a healthy, high-performing board of directors. Their structure is a blueprint model for how board members sing their notes in harmony with the rest of the organization. It creates a great vibe in an organization.

Overseeing the Senior Leader and Board Chair Duet

Who sings lead in a nonprofit organization or a church congregation isn't necessarily a complicated question. It depends on "the song" you are singing at the moment. When it comes to singing lead on the board, it should be the board chair. When it comes to the day-to-day leadership of the organization, it must be the senior leader. Sometimes, board members or committee chairs will lead particular events, but those only occur when the board delegates those responsibilities. Before I go on, I believe it is essential that I underscore the relationship between the board chair and the senior leader.

Earlier, I wrote about my incredible board chairperson partnerships. I took over the lead pastor role in one of the largest congregations in our denomination when I was in my early thirties. Had it not been for Bob Jones, my wise and patient board chair, I would have undoubtedly failed to meet the challenges I faced.

When grading pastors, most people lean toward their ability to communicate. My former pastor and good friend Kevin Murphy contends that "preaching is 90% of a pastor's grade, but only 10% of his actual responsibilities." That might be an understatement.

Bob was a senior staff member at a large corporation working on cutting-edge technology that saved his company over a billion dollars annually. Despite his day job responsibilities, Bob found a way to provide the kind of partnership critical to my development and the growth of our ministry. He found ways to help me navigate the facility, financial, and staff challenges we faced.

Scott Walker replaced Bob as church chairperson, and he taught me the importance of maintaining regular meetings with each other to process what needed to be accomplished at the board level. He was careful to avoid stepping into the day-to-day operations of the ministry.

Bob helped me work through a crisis when we had missed several mortgage payments on our building. It was a purchase we made prematurely. We were over our heads in no time. We would have lost our property if it had not been for a denomination that believed in our vision. I would have lost my mind if it had not been for Bob's steady hand!

Years later, when our congregation was financially stable, we had the opportunity to lead a three-night, county-wide evangelism effort. As chairperson, Scott led our board to support the event. It gave me the authority to sign every financial agreement and contract, making our congregation legally responsible for the event sponsored by only a few participating congregations and three nights of love offerings.

The expenses grew to twice the budgeted amount I had anticipated, and various circumstances caused some congregations to renege on their pledges. We were facing a sizable shortfall, and I realized we would need much more in the love offerings to cover the gap.

Scott offered encouragement and reassurance to the remaining board members. Together, we focused the board on the purpose behind the event and reminded them that God owned the cattle on a thousand hills. All he had to do was to sell a few cows, and we would be okay.

The event went off seamlessly, and nearly one thousand people decided to follow Jesus over the three nights. In addition, the offerings were higher than anticipated. A week after the event, I met with the associate director of the outdoor amphitheater where we held the event. He had initially opposed our using their facility. He told me what enthusiastic feedback he received from all of his staff.

As I got up to leave, he held his hand to shake mine and smiled. He said, "I was wrong about you guys. I have something to give you."

He handed me an envelope and said, "This is a check. It turns out we overcharged you." Then he chuckled before adding, "We overcharge many people. We want you to have this."

I waited to get back to my office before I opened it. The amount of the reimbursement put us $4.00 in the black."

I couldn't wait to tell Scott. He responded, "God is showing off."

I don't know if God ever shows off. But he shows up. He has shown up in my life in great board chairpersons like Bob, Scott, and Ron Knapp. These kinds of partnerships can never be underestimated in their value to the success of nonprofit organizations and church congregations!

Bob, Scott, and Ron never veered into the day-to-day responsibilities of the organizations I led. Neither did they try and control "how" I led. They were honest with me, sometimes appropriately brutally frank with me. They were great examples of bringing the love, being honest, and singing harmoniously.

I did not have to be reminded that I was accountable to the board of directors. But it was secondary to the genuine partnership I forged with the great chairpersons I was fortunate to work with.

Overseeing the Manager is About Singing Harmony		
The Notes of the Senior Leader	**The Notes of the Board Chair**	**The Notes of the Board Member**
Day-to-day operations	Chair board meetings	Fulfills the oversight responsibilities of the Rhythm of Oversight, including: • Mission • Management (including Senior Leader) • Money • Messaging
Hires, supervises, evaluates, and if needed, fires staff	Establishes the agenda for board meetings (in cooperation with the senior leader)	The board hires, manages, and, if need be, fires the senior leader
Leads the day-to-day actions that help implement the mission of the organization	Holds other board members accountable for their commitments	Approves the annual budget, monitors expenses and income, and approves expenditures over any agreed-upon amount.

Responsible for making sure that volunteers are recruited, trained, equipped, empowered, supported, developed, and deployed in a way that grows the organization and advances its impact	Heads the evaluation process of the senior leader	Provides leadership regarding fundraising and is responsible for fulfilling agreed-upon expectations regarding personal giving and personal involvement in raising funds
Forms and maintains a healthy working partnership with the board chairperson.	Serves as the liaison between the senior leader and the board	Responsible for communicating decisions to interested parties with One Voice
Makes sure that the donor base is effectively managed, and new donors are added regularly	Meets regularly with the senior leader	Oversees all legal responsibilities and, in its fiduciary role, is authorized to represent the organization in all legal matters.
Is knowledgeable of the organization's financial health and oversees day-to-day finances following the working budget		Accountable to the rest of the board of directors
Accountable to the entire board of directors	Accountable to the entire board of directors	Accountable to the entire board of directors

Oversight Three
Money

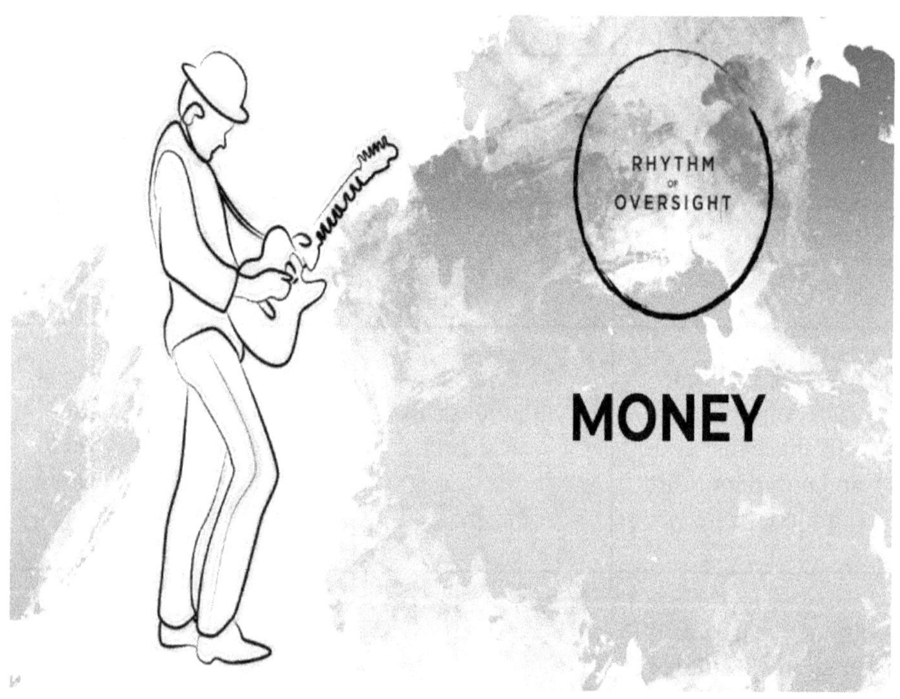

Chapter 9
The Oversight of Money...
Doing Away with Donors

No one has ever become poor by giving.

- Anne Frank

*If you think you are too small to make a difference,
you haven't spent the night with a mosquito.*

- African Proverb

JESUS TALKED MORE ABOUT MONEY than heaven and hell combined. So does a board of directors; talk about money, that is. Outside of providing oversight on the organization's mission, perhaps the most spiritual oversight responsibility a board carries concerns the financial health and performance of the organization.

To any organization, money is a lot like oxygen. It is likely the only thing you can think of when you do not have it, and the feeling is suffocating. Business leaders understand this. If a company does not perform financially, complex and sometimes painful decisions must be made, and people can lose their livelihoods. Ministry leaders must understand that business individuals and ministry people tend to approach finances differently.

Ministry leaders pray as if the solution is all up to God. They tend to start with prayer.

When faced with a challenge, business leaders tend to go into immediate solution mode, including strategizing an answer to the challenge. It is not that they do not trust God, they simply have a different starting point: planning and taking immediate action steps.

The starting point tends to be different, if not the polar opposite. Regarding board meetings, different perspectives will coexist in varying stages of challenges, decisions, and obstacles. This creates the opportunity for "iron to sharpen iron" and to work from both ends of the perspective. Since boards do not meet daily (some meet only once a quarter), frustration can build as people wait to get on the same page.

Both perspectives are needed. Saint Ignatius once said, "Pray as though everything depended on God, and function as if everything depended on you."

Money and ministry. Some people function as if they are strange bedfellows. It isn't easy to achieve results without the two coming together. In my experience:

> Money follows vision.
> Money empowers purpose.
> Money fuels mission.

Money is not evil. Paul said the "love of money" is. Money is neutral, and it is often a necessary part of ministry. God instructs us to be good stewards of it —individually and corporately, including faith-based boards of directors.

When our oldest son Colin married, he and his bride Jess were already full-time missionaries working at the Youth with a Mission base in Kona, Hawaii. They were facing the challenge of fundraising, which included raising all their travel expenses. Because of their ministry responsibilities, their travel is extensive, and the cost is enormous.

Colin and I discussed their fundraising plan several years ago. He smiled and said, "Dad, I know that if you had it, you would just write a check to cover it all."

I replied, "Not a chance."

He was puzzled. My response could be considered unsupportive or as not believing in their ministry. I explained. "I wouldn't want to rob you of all the times when God will come through for you and do so at the very last moment. It is a great way to build your faith muscles. So no, I wouldn't write that check."

I have had so many of these moments that I have lost count. But the stories never get old, and I never take them for granted.

In the faith-based ministry world, God often uses money to increase our dependence upon him. The truth is that wise leadership at the staff and board level depends on God during the planning, implementation, and evaluation phases. I have never found a part of a ministry where I am not entirely dependent on God's guidance and empowerment to produce the desired results.

Clarifying Financial Expectations

Before a board of directors can oversee its organization's finances, the members must clearly understand what is expected of them. The board's fiduciary responsibility is to fulfill its financial obligations to the organization it oversees.

This means fulfilling board duties of care by constantly being aware of financial affairs and being updated regarding its current financial needs and obligations. A board must act in a fiscally responsible way and always make financial decisions that benefit the organization and not any board member. Finally, the board meets its duty of obedience by using its available resources to advance its mission.

In most nonprofit organizations and church congregation board meetings, dedicated time is allotted to review the organization's financial affairs. It is worth repeating that a board member does not have to be a finance expert. Still, she needs to be able to read and understand the financial reports prepared for the board and make solid decisions in this crucial oversight area.

There is another dicey element to how organizations place responsibility on board members in the financial area. It is more personal and deals with clarifying what is expected from board members regarding their financial contribution and involvement in raising funds for the organization.

This is deeply personal because it addresses a member's time and money.

A board member should never be surprised by an unexpected fundraising obligation. The Lord loves a cheerful giver, but I've never heard someone let out a cheerful yelp when a financial requirement is unsuspectingly sprung on them, an approach guaranteed to create division and toxicity in the boardroom.

I once consulted with a nonprofit whose funding model was minimally dependent on donations, including individual, corporate, or foundations. The senior leader asked me to help him recruit new board members. I inquired about his specific expectations for each board member regarding raising funds. He was clear, "We are fee-based regarding revenue. Board members won't have to do any fundraising."

Given the clarity, I recruited three new members who brought much-needed skills to his board. You can imagine my surprise when he began the orientation session for new members with the amount of donated revenue expected each board member to raise.

This senior leader didn't just lack clarity in this one area. He often switched strategies in staff and board meetings without any input from anyone else. Not surprisingly, none of the three new members completed their first three-year term on his board.

Expectations matter!

The Oversight of Money

My executive director in my early days of Youth for Christ was Don Mardock. Don once told me, "You can delegate authority, but you cannot delegate responsibility." While a board of directors may charge the senior leader, a director of development, or its finance committee with the function of fundraising, the primary responsibility to maintain a healthy financial state rests solely with the board of directors. If an organization continually struggles with raising adequate funds, the board might ask itself, "Who hired the senior leader?" or "Who approved the director of the development's plan?" The board should ask, "What will we do to correct this issue?"

Regarding fundraising, the board must consider its role in leading the efforts because it is ultimately responsible for the organization's financial performance. You will recall that the Boys and Girls Clubs of Oakland had specific hours and roles each board member committed to fulfilling yearly. There were clear expectations. Some organizations have a minimum requirement board members are expected to contribute and/or raise.

In your present board situation, can you answer these two questions:

What am I expected to contribute to the organization financially?

What role do I have in fundraising for the organization?

The board and senior leader must clarify everyone's responsibilities in this area. Even if there aren't any financial "giving or getting" commitments, it is still a good practice for board members to connect their network of family members, friends, and associates to the organization they oversee. This can occur by introducing your network to the senior leader or the board chairperson or inviting your connections to a fundraising or an open event. I have taken the opportunity to invite my friends to an informal lunch with the senior leader or another board member. When I do, I tell my friend precisely how they might be able to help the organization, and I mention the opportunity to contribute financial support.

Each board member should stay on top of how the organization implements its mission and know how that impacts the clientele it serves.

Put Your Money Where Your Mission Is

I have been a part of an incredible nonprofit organization called the Leadership Connection since its inception. Its founder and president, Neil Sullivan, and I have known each other since Neil was a junior in high school and was a member of my YMCA youth group. TLC's mission is to "support and strengthen kingdom leaders to help them achieve their call to its fullest potential." I have had the privilege of facilitating three separate groups for over ten years.

I began taking an informal and very unscientific poll of my TLC pastor groups by asking them, "What percentage of your annual budget do you estimate goes towards supporting your Sunday morning services operations (i.e., facilities, staffing, curriculum, programming, etc.)?"

The feedback was astonishing to me. The lowest percentage of a congregation's annual budget supporting Sunday services was 40%, while the highest was 90%. The average was well over two-thirds of a congregation's income devoted to sustaining the activities on the church campus on Sunday mornings.

My follow-up question was, "How many of you consider your mission aligned with the Great Commission?" Nine out of every ten pastors told me they did!

My point? Does a church that claims its mission to be "go and make disciples" yet spends most of its time and money on Sunday services pass the sniff test of being a Great Commission Church? (I will let you answer that question.) Had all of the congregation's board members spent time comparing their church's mission metrics to where it spent the most time and money, many would have made serious adjustments to what they were doing or not doing.

This is one of the prime oversight responsibilities of a board of directors. It is why a board must have a set of metrics, a scoreboard to review each time it meets to gauge if the organization is executing the cause it claims to exist to advance.

The board is responsible for ensuring that the organization puts its money where its mission is!

Faith-based senior leaders need the board's oversight to ensure they stay on mission. Boards are in place to oversee the investment of finances given to the organization to fulfill the cause we promote to our members and donors. I repeat:

Money follows vision.

Money empowers purpose.

Money fuels mission.

To be effective financial overseers, board members must know how the organization performs regarding its stated mission. It makes it easier to ask for support from friends, family, and associates when the organization you serve is equipping you to tell a convincing narrative where mission and execution often cross paths.

A New Fundraising Approach: Do Away with Donors!

Many people will tell you that the secret to fundraising in the ministry world lies in one area: relationships.

While much is to be said and applauded about taking a relational approach to fundraising, there is more to consider than just making a friend. Nonprofits must create a paradigm shift in how they relate to the people who support their efforts. It begins with the way we describe them. Instead of referring to them as donors, contributors, or giving units, they should be seen as investors. The reason for the shift is more than semantics.

People think differently when investing in an opportunity or a cause rather than donating to it. Being referred to as an investor invokes different emotions from being viewed as a donor or contributor.

People who make significant gifts (large donors) carry an added burden. They know how much impact the size of their contribution can make in an organization's effort to execute its mission and achieve its goals and objectives. They also know that choosing to give to a particular organization means they won't be giving to other deserving causes.

They carry the burden of stewardship. That is why significant givers approach their donations more as investors than donors. They need to be treated as such.

What Do People Invest In?

People donate to organizations. But investors invest in three things:

- People
- Purpose or causes (think mission)
- Potential or proven outcomes

The first thing that stewards invest in is people. When missiologists study the missional movement, they observe that people join missional communities for three reasons. First, they like the leader and want to have a relationship with him. Second, they like the people in the group and enjoy being in the community with everyone. They enjoy being with the people who make up the community. Finally, they are committed to the group's cause or mission.

When attracting investors who will devote their time or money to your organization, you can never underestimate the value of having good people in key leadership roles. I cannot tell you how many times I have attended a fundraising event solely because of a friend's invitation or because I liked and respected the nonprofit's senior leader (or another key staff member).

People support people they trust, and they give to organizations with leaders they respect and admire.

A second reason people invest in is a vital purpose or cause. Investing is different from donating. People donate to charities. There are many reasons why people donate money. Sometimes people contribute to a charity because it makes them feel good about themselves. Science indicates that dopamine is released when people feel good about themselves based on the choices they make. Other times, people might give money out of obligation. And sometimes people donate money to get someone off their back. That sounds crude, but it's true.

Investing is different. An investment is deliberate. And there is usually a sound reason behind it. One of those reasons is the person who is leading the organization, and the second reason is because of what the organization is doing.

Think of it this way. Have you ever watched the evening news and suddenly found yourself emotionally moved by a story about suffering, injustice, or rescue? One moment, you are watching the weather patterns; the next moment, you are moved to tears by a story that captivates your emotions.

Multiple reasons might explain the tears or strong emotions. Still, it likely has to do more with a particular experience you have had in life.

You are drawn to causes that address those issues. Keep in mind, there are many people willing to invest in the mission your organization exists to fulfill.

Give people who resonate with your cause a reason to invest in your organization. They are not likely to make an investment that is purely personality-driven and dependent on an individual. Be clear about your mission and be sure to have current examples demonstrating how you are living it.

To draw investors, not just donors, you must have strong people in your organization who help drive its purpose and mission. A third component investors pay attention to is the likelihood that one's investment will produce the difference someone wants to make. Consider the following two questions:

- What potential does an organization possess?
- What are the proven outcomes an organization has to show for the resources people have already provided?

The first question is often asked about a start-up organization. I vividly recall when Neil Sullivan and I were preparing to launch The Leadership Connection. We didn't have a proven track record. We didn't have a history at all.

We invited a small group of our friends to attend an introductory meeting so we could pitch the idea. We knew a few of them could help us bootstrap the venture. As we prepared for the meeting, I recall one of us saying, "We don't have any steak to sell. All we have is sizzle."

We used that exact line in the meeting, and it resonated with our friends. We honestly explained the results we believed we would obtain by launching the ministry. We also were honest about our lack of proof, but the people in the room believed in our ability to do what we promised.

We took in enough investment to launch TLC for its inaugural year. Recently the organization celebrated its seventeenth year in ministry in the United States and abroad. Proof of concept!

Our friends invested in the potential of the mission of TLC. Their confidence was based on two things: we had a track record as proven leaders, and the early investors believed in the organization's mission.

When an organization has been around for a few years, savvy investors will often look to see if it has proof of outcomes. In other words, does it deliver on its focused ministry promises? Long-term success is vital to investors, especially if they plan to invest significantly.

Remember, when someone invests a large amount of money into one organization, other well-deserving causes will receive less or sometimes nothing. That brings the focus of stewardship into play. Friends of mine who have the gift of giving also have the discernment that comes with it.

Accounting for Investments
Made to Your Organization

Sometimes organizations need to do a better job of being accountable to contributors and investors. They don't show proper gratitude for the support they receive. Have you ever attended a nonprofit's fundraising dinner and contributed, only to have your donation ignored? Sometimes you don't hear from anyone in the organization again until you get invited to their next money-raising event. It makes you feel like Dana Carvey's old Church Lady character from *Saturday Night Live* who liked to say, "Now isn't that special!"

Contributions and investments alike need to be treated with grateful acknowledgment. Significant investments need to include more. Investments require accountability.

Earlier in this book, when I referred to the Young Life organization, I noted that around a quarter of a million teenagers attend one of the 26 Young Life camps. It is one of the most successful camp ministries in the entire world. But Young Life has learned as much about fundraising as they have camping in its 80-year history. The organization does a stellar job raising funds through serious investors to build new conference grounds. One of the commitments they have made to their investors is that they will only break ground on a new conference center once all of the necessary funds are committed. In most cases, a shovel will only touch dirt once $35,000,000 has been donated or pledged.

Young Life calls this their "Campership Legacy Fund." It is designed to "reach thousands of kids, one at a time." Their promise to their investors is that the fund will be well-managed (by outside professionals) and there will be total transparency. All the performance data and information regarding the fund is available to the investors and can be reviewed at any time. Now here's the thing: they deliver on their promise!

Does your organization excel at being accountable to your investors and contributors? Do you have the means to let people know the score regarding the execution of your mission?

As the former co-managing partner of the San Francisco Bay Area Barnabas Group, I was exposed to multiple nonprofit organizations. At each of our meetings, we had three nonprofits make presentations where they shared their mission and the impact they were making. I was always most moved by the ones that could succinctly share with our audience the impact they were having in foster care, homelessness, eradicating disease, human trafficking, and evangelizing unchurched GenZers and Millennials.

The one thing these particular nonprofits had in common was that their metrics communicated to those listening "what the score was" regarding their intended purpose and their progress in fulfilling it.

Does your organization communicate how you are doing to your investors and contributors regarding mission impact? Do they look at you as a wise investment?

I am glad business professionals take the time to serve on nonprofit and congregational boards. They think differently. They scrutinize the numbers more carefully. They ask questions and are fearless of being held accountable for the organization's financial performance. Businesspeople live in a world of metrics. They are familiar with terms like monetize, deliverables, margins, contributing, operating, gross, and KPIs, which are not widely used in ministry. Business is a world where numbers tell stories, and people are often held accountable for achieving them. The nonprofit world operates lesser like that, and the church sphere even to a lesser degree.

Investors scour numbers carefully. They do the same when deciding whether to support a nonprofit or a congregation. It is up to faith-based organizations to provide accurate metrics to explain the likelihood that the investors' gift will be used wisely.

The more accountable you are willing to be to your financial supporter, the more likely you will be able to build and grow an extensive database of serious investors to fuel your mission.

Fundraising

It would be wrong to include a chapter on the board's responsibility for overseeing money and not say anything about raising it. Let me say this upfront. Whether or not the board has any agreed-upon involvement regarding fundraising, the board is solely responsible for overseeing the strategy, goals, objectives, and outcomes of any fundraising efforts. If the senior leader is charged with fundraising, the board still oversees the senior leader. If there is a director of development responsible for raising money, it is still the board that oversees the senior leader whose job is to oversee the director of development. If a finance committee has been tasked with raising funds, who appointed the members of the committee?

Do you see where I am going with this? The board is not necessarily responsible for every fundraising activity, but the board is responsible for the organization's financial health – hard stop.

If you need clarification, reread the previous sentence.

The board does not have the luxury of sitting back and pointing fingers at someone's failure to raise money. The board is charged with this oversight responsibility.

There is significant competition when raising money for your nonprofit or congregation. Remember, there are roughly one-and-a-half million nonprofit organizations, and over 300,000 are churches where many people are used to giving regularly.

The good news is that our country is very generous. A typical citizen gives to four-and-a-half organizations a year. Many people would gladly support your organization if they knew who you were and what you did.

It's up to your organization to identify potential supporters and to build and maintain a relationship with them. It is up to your board to oversee that it happens. Let me give you a few simple steps you can take to build and maintain your donor and investor list.

Step One: Have everyone in the organization compile a list of personal contacts they know who might be interested in what your ministry is doing. Have them include the names, addresses (especially email), and phone numbers (especially cell phones) of each person, couple, church congregation, and company.

Step Two: Assign someone the task of compiling the information into a database you can use to inform people about who you are, what your mission is, and what you are doing to advance your mission in the community. This is also a way to have a ready-made audience you can alert when you have events open to the public or fundraising opportunities you would like them to attend, like a gala or a golf tournament.

Step Three: Continuously add new names to your database and treat them with the importance they deserve. I have a friend who ran a nonprofit organization for nearly twenty years, but he never grew his database to over one hundred and twenty names. He received a generous gift from a foundation and made it last for years. Eventually, the unwillingness to take the nonprofit's database seriously led them to close the organization. It was a loss for the entire community.

Step Four: You must answer how you will utilize your database. Here are some ways:

- Communicate to your database about who you are and what you are about. This sounds like an oversimplification, but it is Basic Communication 101! The rule of thumb is to overcommunicate!

- Use your database as a means of recruiting volunteers to meet the various opportunities your organization provides as well as meet the needs you will have.

- Use your database to invite people you know to events your organization is hosting, like fundraising dinners, golf tournaments, and activities the public can attend without being in the way of ministry.

Your database should include every past, present, and potential donor and investor you can think of. They should receive every pertinent marketing piece you produce. Every marketing piece should be targeted to reach your audience. Make it as laser-focused as possible.

Give Here... and Here... and Here... and...

There are many ways to raise funding for your organization. Let's start with a simple Give Here button on your website. It should stand out, and the process should be simple and safe to give. Online giving should have the option to give regularly, which is a baby step to helping donors become potential investors. It would be best to have mobile-friendly possibilities, including giving by texting.

In the 21st Century, many safe and convenient methods exist to give to a cause that matters. Most financial support came from the Builder and Boomer generations not long ago. Have you stopped considering that the Millennial and GenZ generations are no longer in preschool and daycare? The older GenZers and Millennials are in high-capacity jobs in the workforce, and Millennials are in their forties. In comparison, the older GenZers are 25 years old. These two generations are cause-driven and tech-savvy. They don't usually write checks!

Events are a great way to draw a crowd and tell your story. Whether a luncheon, a living room dessert, a fundraising gala, or a golf tournament, events can raise awareness of your organization and money to help address its needs.

It's Not What You Know But Who You Know

There is no magic wand to wave guaranteed to provide the support of foundations or grant providing organizations. The road to those types of financial support is clearly marked: "Personal Relationships. If you have the time and patience, gaining support from them is an excellent way of raising financial support.

Generally, relationships within foundations take time to build enough trust to garner support. Such support will likely begin at a smaller amount. If your organization demonstrates good stewardship with its entrusted funds, it can build over time.

Where Will Your Support Come From?

Funding can come from so many different areas, including:

- Foundations and grant providers
- Individuals, both small donations and significant investments (don't forget to make it safe and easy to give)
- Events like the ones already mentioned and others like online auctions, virtual gatherings, hybrid gatherings (in-person and online), events

where you charge admission, and anything other than bake sales and car washes
- Campaigns and capital campaigns
- The old-fashioned person-to-person meeting

I recently met with a new executive director who was struggling with the need to double her organization's budget. One of her well-meaning board members suggested they aggressively go after church support. I winced, and she picked up on it and later asked about my reaction.

I explained to her that churches are also nonprofit organizations. They have missions to fulfill. They have financial commitments, including a list of organizations they already support. My counsel to her and to you is that unless you have a strong relationship with someone in a decision-making position, the likelihood of receiving significant support from a church congregation is the same as from a foundation where you don't know anyone.

When I was the interim director of the Oakland Youth and Children's nonprofit, the board charged me with garnering significant church support. It wasn't that churches didn't appreciate what we were doing; their mission budgets were almost already committed beyond their means. I recently came across one of our old annual budget's year-to-date reports. I calculated that 3.8% of our nearly one-million-dollar annual budget came from church congregations. It isn't that churches don't want to help. Remember, most of them are facing their own revenue challenges.

Do Not Neglect to Ask

I don't care if you are approaching a foundation for a sizeable grant, a corporation for a substantial donation, or standing at the podium and asking dinner guests to provide for your organization's financial needs, you've got to be willing to ask for what the organization needs.

Nonprofit leaders and pastors possess different skills and gifts when raising funds. Another quality supplied in varying amounts is courage. Many funding opportunities never materialize because the person doesn't have the moxie to ask people to invest in the cause.

I don't blame you if you think I'm joking. I'm not. When I was in my early twenties, a board member once told me my executive director had met with him. He said, "I knew he was going to ask me for a sizeable donation." He then let out a long sigh before he added, "When he got around to asking me, the amount he asked me was so low that I couldn't write the check fast enough. I was prepared to give him at least ten times that amount if he had had the guts to ask."

You've got to ask for what you need. If you don't believe in the mission, who will?

I have been to several fundraising galas that turned into friend-raising events because the person in charge of the call to action made a weak request for financial support. I attended such an event with over two hundred people present. There were pledge cards in the center of every table. Those present enjoyed an excellent program. They all knew they were attending a fundraising event. The board chairperson concluded the evening by saying, "I hope we have made many friends tonight. Thank you for coming." He neglected to invite anyone to invest in our mission. One of my guests tracked me down in the parking lot to give me a sizeable gift. I was convinced many more like him wanted to support the mission and be a part of the solution.

You've got to ask.

If you can believe it, the same organization did the same thing the following year. They turned a fundraising event into a fund-losing one two years in a row! The two events cost over $30,000 in total.

Finally, I once flew over 2,000 miles to attend the launch of a good friend's international nonprofit. Its focus was to promote training opportunities for Palestinian teenagers from different racial, political, and religious backgrounds. They would fly to America, be hosted in Christian homes, and learn how to build relationships, heal hurts, understand one another, and discover how to reconcile their differences – even though many of the political leaders in their land had not.

We spent three days meeting with the Mayor Pro Tem of Jerusalem, two members of his cabinet, and influential Muslim and Christian business professionals. Most of them had relocated to America from Middle Eastern countries. My friend sought their support for bringing fifty teenagers over the following summer for a two-week trial program.

During these gatherings, I was introduced to a new saying: "It all started when he hit me back." It didn't make much sense when I first heard it, but as the meetings went on, I soon discovered it explained much about Middle Eastern culture.

The meetings saw significant breakthroughs, and there was the likelihood that the following summer would see the first actual trial run for the program.

Our last evening together, my faith-filled friend had planned a fundraising gala attended by over 300 people in the Chicagoland area. The program featured testimonies from a group of students who had participated in a ten-person pilot program the previous summer. The Jerusalem Mayor Pro Tem gave his enthusiastic unofficial commitment to do his part. The most influential Muslim leader in the area pledged to fly to Jerusalem to meet with the mayor to work through the details.

All that was left was for my friend to ask those attending the Gala for the needed finances to make it happen.

Pledge cards, envelopes, and pens were in the center of the tables. Everyone knew they were at a fundraising event. It had communicated what the event was for on the invitations.

After all the speakers had given terrific presentations, my friend got up to conclude the evening. He thanked everyone for coming and closed in prayer. "Good night, everyone," he said. "Thank you for coming."

The people got up and headed to their cars. I sat stunned. Great crowd. Great atmosphere. An excellent heartfelt program.

Then, goodnight.

There was no ask!

No kidding!

Most people left immediately. Some lingered. Some had already written checks and even searched to find someone they could leave it with. They were sold on the mission even though no one had to ask them to invest in it.

I wish I could tell you it did not happen, but it did. It was the worst request for financial support I ever witnessed. I knew my friend believed in his mission. But he whiffed when asking others to believe along with him.

That night he laid his nonprofit organizational dream to rest. It stayed on life support for another year, but it never recovered. Years later, the meeting in Jerusalem with the mayor and businessman has yet to materialize. I couldn't blame anyone. They couldn't be expected to believe in the mission more than the founder did.

One way to get past the awkwardness of asking donors to give is to realize they should be treated as something other than donors. Treat them like investors by providing them with a compelling reason to participate in the ministry your organization is providing.

Money is like oxygen. At the event in Chicago, it felt like someone sucked the air out of the room and my friend's dream suffocated to death.

It did not have to. The outcome could have been much different if my friend had a board of directors comprised of vibrant leaders ready to help him overcome his reluctance to ask. Walt Disney once said, "If you can dream it, you can do it." But you still have to pay for it. In the faith-based world of nonprofits, somebody has to ask the investors to join the cause.

Have conviction. Be daring. Invite people to invest. Be inspiring and present a compelling cause.

For the sake of the organization, do not neglect to ask!

Oversight Four

Messaging

Chapter 10
Meetings and Messaging (Part One)...
Making Them Matter

How good and pleasant it is when God's people live together in unity.

> - Psalm 133:1

Question: How many board members does it take to change a lightbulb?

Answer: One, but only after the entire board decides to change it.

IT'S EIGHT O'CLOCK IN THE MORING, and almost half of the members have wandered into the conference room. The meeting was supposed to have started already, but it was a casual group led by a preoccupied chairperson and a senior leader who led by accident. Most people on the board anticipated the meeting would start slowly and its pace would lessen to a painful crawl within about twenty minutes. When the members finally sat down, they would be given the minutes from the last meeting and a single-page financial report that didn't resemble anything someone would receive in an ordinary business meeting.

The chairperson began the meeting by 8:17, and he mumbled a quick opening prayer. Then he waited for everyone to read the minutes. Since there were no amendments, they went on to the financial report. You could summarize the information by saying, "We've got too many bills and not enough cash to meet them."

Then the chairperson asked if anyone had anything to discuss. He referred to it as a team approach to creating the meeting agenda. The remaining part of the meeting boiled down to a free-for-all ad hoc discussion resulting in no action being taken. The meeting stretched out to fill the allotted ninety minutes.

The board chair adjourned the meeting at precisely 9:30 by asking the senior leader to close in prayer. As they made their way to their cars, one of the more polite members was overheard mumbling, "That's ninety minutes of my life I'll never get back."

Is it any wonder that meetings have a reputation for being a waste of time? At least in this illustration, no one was hurt in the making of the board meeting. Sometimes people do get hurt.

Board Member Gone Wild

A few years ago, a pastor friend of mine was shepherding a church that had endured its share of difficulties over an extended period. Some were relational in nature; there was a shortage of volunteers, and financial resources were hard to secure. In confidence, he told me he often felt alone and without much support or help from his board of directors.

However, he was hoping to get some good news from the board treasurer at the next board meeting. The treasurer had met with their property owner in hopes of renegotiating the lease.

Instead of being presented with a reduced lease, the pastor listened as his treasurer took a deep dive into the congregation's finances. The financial report quickly morphed into the treasurer's commentary on the state of the church. He said, "The property owner is still considering our request, but I don't think it matters. In reality, we must make some serious reductions in our spending. As board treasurer, it is my responsibility to manage our finances. I have made every cut in expenses, including the pastor's salary. I've decided we must reduce his salary by forty percent. This action is effective immediately. By immediately, I mean tonight. I will announce this decision next Sunday at church and send out a letter informing the congregation the next day. Here is the letter I'll be mailing."

Most troubling, the treasurer assumed authority he did not have and the rest of the board let him. No one, not even the board chairperson, pushed back. No one bothered to ask a question. The pastor tried to object, but the treasurer mumbled something about a conflict of interest and dismissed his objection.

The treasurer's plan was executed, and he made the announcement the following Sunday morning. Less than two months later, the board chair announced that the pastor was leaving.

Three months later, the church closed.

Dysfunction thrives in an atmosphere where confusion and weak leadership go unaddressed. I am not suggesting the decision and results would have been different if the board had interacted collaboratively and engaged in spirited discussion to find alternate solutions. But by allowing everyone, including the pastor, to weigh in with their perspectives, opinions, and viewpoints, the board would have achieved a level of buy-in towards the final adoption of the best possible approach to their dilemma. Even more disturbing is that no one stopped to pray and seek God's direction.

Better Ways to Work Together

The treasurer assumed authority to make financial decisions on the board's behalf, and the chairperson's weak leadership empowered him to create and implement a decision that led to the church's closure. As far as the congregation understood, the treasurer had the authority to act and speak on behalf of the board and them. Trust in the board's guidance declined, and morale dropped rapidly.

There is a way to achieve better outcomes. I recently had the pleasure of working with Benjie Craig, the chairperson of his congregation's board, as he led them through the rigorous process of selecting a new pastor. Pastoral transitions are often painful. During the process, Sunday attendance drops, as does giving, and the volunteer base suffers. Morale sinks, motivation wanes, and mission often gets blurred, if not altogether ignored.

Several factors made this particular search a challenging one. It was the congregation's third change of lead pastor in just over a decade. It was during the Covid pandemic. Because the church was independent, it had no denomination to assist it. Finally, its location in the Silicon Valley of San Francisco made it difficult to attract candidates who would view buying a home there as a significant stumbling block.

But the critical difference is that Benjie led. He involved every member of the board as well as past members. They first had to find and select a Christian executive search firm. There were a lot of forms to fill out and profiles to create. Benjie quipped, "I never did online dating, but I think I'm beginning to feel what it is like for people who do."

Once they decided which search firm to use, they developed a congregational profile. It was an honest portrayal of who they were, one designed to appeal to candidates looking for a challenge.

All the board members were engaged in the process, resulting in over two hundred applicants. The search firm used the profile to narrow the search down to six highly qualified applicants. The board authorized Benjie and another member to conduct the initial interviews with the half-dozen candidates and make recommendations for three applicants to visit the church over three separate weekends.

If you've ever been a part of a pastoral search team, you'll recognize that I'm only giving you selected highlights. The process had its ups and downs and several false starts. When they thought they had narrowed the list to three final candidates, one announced he had accepted a call to another congregation.

By the time Chairperson Craig stood before the congregation to make the official announcement of the new pastor, there had been hundreds of behind-the-scenes phone calls, emails, videos produced, profiles created, budget adjustments, resumes scoured, and individual and group prayer times. There were hours of hard work, spirited debate, disagreements, research, and countless meetings. When Benjie made the announcement, he brought the entire board upfront to acknowledge that it was a team effort and to share both the moment and the credit.

In the end, all of those meetings were worth it. Even the frustrating ones.

Meetings are a Petri Dish for BOARDom

The humor columnist Dave Berry once wrote, "If you had to identify in one word, the reason why the human race has not achieved, and never will achieve its full potential, that word would be meetings." If I were to share the comment in any corporate office in America, I would surely get a few hearty "Amens!"

Please glance at the text box on page 195 to see what people say about meetings. Meetings are the petri dish from whence BOARDom emerges. If people want to create boredom, frustration, confusion, and disengagement, all they need to do is call a meeting.

Many people deplore meetings, no matter how important or necessary they might be. As a person rises in her industry, meetings become a significant part of her daily schedule.

Church and nonprofit organizations are no different. There are lots of meetings, including board meetings.

But here lies the problem and the challenge: meetings are not the issue! Bad meetings are! I have an idea for a solution. Hear me out. Let's make meetings better, and let's make meetings matter!

MAKING BETTER MEETINGS THAT MATTER!

Until recently, I had lived my entire life in the San Francisco Bay Area. I was afforded the opportunity to see some of the greatest athletes in the history of college and professional sports: Willie Mays, Joe Montana, Rick Berry, the Bash Brothers, and the Splash Brothers.

All athletes have one thing in common. They all warm up to prepare to play a game. It was worth the price of admission to watch Reggie Jackson launch batting practice baseballs into the stratosphere and a delight to observe Wardell Stephen Curry II shoot from the rafters before a game.

All competitors who want to perform at their best acknowledge the importance of their pregame routines. The same is true regarding having better board meetings. I firmly believe that no one ever outgrows the basics, but we ignore them to our detriment.

Have you ever considered that the primary reason meetings are so bad is a result of how little attention is paid to the pre-meeting routines? My son Cameron is a high school basketball coach, and he puts more thought and preparation into a game plan for teenage boys than most executives or board chairpersons put into planning their next meeting.

If you want better meetings, I believe you have to give attention and time to these three aspects:

- The Planning and Preparation Stage of the Meeting
- The Operational Stage of the Meeting
- The Follow Through Stage of the Meeting

Stage One: Planning and Preparation

When one stops to consider that nearly two-thirds of the 11 million meetings in America daily are conducted without an agenda, it isn't tricky to figure out why meetings are boring and unproductive. Better meetings start with better *planning and preparation*.

Step One: Determine the Intended Outcomes You Want to Achieve at the Next Meeting. When it comes to leading any meeting, I like to start with the end result in mind. It is essential for each participant to be clear about the desired outcomes to achieve at the upcoming meeting. Everyone should understand what issues must be addressed and what decisions must be made. This kind of clarity going into a meeting leads to productive discussions, good decisions, and unambiguous action plans.

Step Two: Develop the Pre-Meeting Packet to be Sent to Each Member at Least Four Days Before the Meeting. This Includes:

- **Previous Meeting Minutes:** Board members need to review the previous minutes of the meeting. If there are any discrepancies found, they will need to be brought up at the upcoming meeting and amended before the minutes are passed and submitted into the record.

- **Financial Reports:** Each nonprofit organization can internally choose what financial reports to address and track. This is part of the board's fiduciary responsibility of the Duty of Care.

The Meeting Problem

There are 11 million meetings each day in America, half of which are deemed a waste of time.

Meeting participants report:

- 63% of meetings don't have an agenda.

- 91% of participants admit to daydreaming

- 73% admit to bringing other work with them.

- 39% admit to falling asleep.

$1 billion is wasted every day in America on useless meetings.

Harvard Business Review reports that 65% of executives say that "Meetings keep them from doing their jobs," and 71% say that "Meetings are a waste of time."

Nonprofits use reports similar to a business Profit and Loss Statement or a Balance Sheet because they have revenue instead of income and track activities instead of profit. I will address this later regarding how to conduct an actual board meeting.

- **Missional Metrics Scoreboard Update:** The board of directors needs to be apprised as to how the organization is performing regarding its stated mission. A board should pay attention to essential metrics and track them on a consistent basis. Financial performance and health are important, but they are not the only metrics to consider. You don't want to be money-rich and mission poor

- **Reports:** Reports submitted by the senior leader, any committee head, or other staff are an efficient use of time and will keep everyone updated on vital organizational activities. The best reports are an opening paragraph, a few bullet points highlighting wins and challenges, and a brief closing paragraph. The longer a report is, the less likely it will be read.

- **Agenda for the Upcoming Meeting:** it is vital to provide a clear agenda communicating what will be covered in the meeting. It should include the headline: *"Intended outcomes of this meeting are_______,"* and include personal check-in, devotional and opening prayer, review and passing of last month's minutes, financial report(s), missional metrics scoreboard, other reports, old business, new business, takeaways, and commitments, and closing prayer. (An Agenda Template is in Appendix E.)

- **Personal Member Commitments Made:** We always encourage every organization we work with to have a rapid "go-around-the-room" and have each participant share their takeaways and commitments from the meeting. This is a great way to cement critical decisions and the organization's challenges or celebrate big or small wins. More importantly, having each participant share their commitment(s) during the meeting on behalf of the organization and the completion date of said commitments. Placing these at the bottom of the agenda of the upcoming meeting is a courteous reminder for anyone that hasn't followed through on what was promised.

- **Prompt Members to Prepare:** Add this phrase at the bottom of the agenda: "Our Duty of Care is to review all materials and come prepared to engage in the work of our organization fully."

Suppose you receive a packet of materials like the one described above four days before the meeting. In that case, you belong to a nonprofit or congregational board in the nation's top ten-perfect prepared organizations (this is an unverified statistic, but according to my experience, it is accurate). Such a high level of preparation signals for everyone to be engaged fully and to bring their best effort to overseeing their organization.

Stage Two: Running a Better Meeting

I hope you haven't skipped this part of the book. If you just read my last sentence, I have hope you will have better-prepared meetings and members. But even after an athlete warms up, she has to play the game.

What follows is a step-by-step basic outline for running a better board meeting.

Welcome and Personal Check-In

It is essential to take the time to let every board member do a quick personal check-in to provide an update about life, especially about anything that is burdening the member, anything likely to keep him from being at his or her absolute best during the meeting. Avoid chit-chat, non-essential details, and limit each check-in to one minute.

State the Outcomes of the Meeting

Samuel Johnson once wrote, "People need to be reminded more than they need to be informed." Meetings earn their "time wasters" reputation because many do not have a good reason to take place. If your board has nothing of consequence to deal with, why not conduct the meeting online in about thirty minutes? You can approve the minutes, review the finances and metrics, and save everyone the frustration of sitting through a purposeless meeting. By answering the question, "What are the intended outcomes of this meeting?" you can protect yourself from: (1) Holding useless meetings, and (2) being able to shorten the meetings to the actual required time to achieve their intended purpose.

Devotion and Opening Prayer

An opening devotional and prayer should mean more than the equivalent of playing the National Anthem before a game. The person assigned this task will do a great service to the other members by paying close attention to the subjects and issues facing the board and finding an appropriate passage tailored to the matters at hand.

Previous Meeting Minutes

Nonprofit organizations are required by law to keep and record the minutes of their board meetings. Some states also require committees to do the same. (Check with your state to make sure you comply). That doesn't mean you must record everything said, but you should provide the

There are only five things that one can do in a meeting:

1. Make a decision.
2. Solve a problem.
3. Exchange Information (including training).
4. Create a plan.
5. Evaluate an outcome.

essential discussions leading to adopting policies or critical decisions.

The previous meeting minutes need to be included in the packet delivered beforehand, and everyone should be familiar with them. The chairperson should ask for any corrections or additions to be made. Once any changes have occurred, a motion, a second, and a vote should be taken to approve them and must be included in your meeting minutes.

Review Reports

There are several reports to review in a board meeting. Let's start with money.

Start with the Financial Report(s)

Most nonprofits and congregations use standard financial reports familiar to the business leaders on their boards. Using internal language like Profit and Loss statements or Balance Sheets is convenient and readily understood by all members. The nonprofit world sometimes employs different names for these reports. A list of four financial statements must be filed annually with the IRS and, for transparency's sake, and make them available to your investors and donors.

Statement of Activities: This tracks what money is left after all expenses are subtracted from the revenue. Revenue includes donations, pledges for future income, program fees, donated materials, membership fees, event revenue, grants, and any other form of revenue. Expenses include rent or mortgage payments, utilities, telephone, equipment, office supplies, payroll, health care, etc. This would be called a Profit and Loss statement for a company.

Statement of Functional Position: This is the nonprofit version of a Balance Sheet and keeps track of assets, liabilities, and net assets. Some investors pay careful attention to this sheet when considering making significant donations to a nonprofit.

Statement of Cash Flow: This report shows how the organization generates and uses cash. It tracks revenue and expenses in operations, investments, and financing.

Statement of Functional Expenses: This shows how expenses are allocated to various programs and functions.

While most nonprofits do not have to pay federal taxes on revenue related to advancing their mission, they must annually file an informational return to the federal government. That submission is referred to as IRS Form 990. It shows the organization's income, expenses, assets, liabilities, and activities. It is wise to make this report available to the public for transparency and integrity, although it does not have to contain the exact details required by the IRS.

A nonprofit or congregation does not have to review each of the above reports every month. But it is the fiduciary responsibility of the board to be aware of the current state of the organization's economic health. The more informed a board is, the more options it may have if and when revenue goes down. Too many boards only have one tool available to use, cutting expenses.

A board should make it a habit to "religiously" review its Statement of Activities every month. In some cases, it is important to include a review of the Statement of Financial Position. The other reports will be helpful to review when more information is required.

As with the minutes, there must be a motion, second, and vote to approve the financial report. All the information should be included in the meeting minutes.

Review the Missional Scoreboard

Studies reveal that the best way to motivate a team toward reaching its goals and objectives is to provide regular updates on what progress is being made. Think back to the Golden State Warriors' metrics when keeping score on how they are advancing their mission. They keep track of things like math problems solved, donated tickets, and meals provided to needy families.

> **DISCLAIMER:**
>
> Perhaps you would argue that I've included too many reports. I don't blame you. Keep in mind many of the reports will contain information a board member would not likely know if they were not submitted in a brief report,
>
> Read them ahead of time and only focus on what is essential to the needs of the organization.

The best boards and senior leaders understand what activities lead to desirable results. Have you ever noticed that baseball managers do not track ticket or hot dog sales, and they ignore attendance? Those activities do not lead to winning baseball games.

What metrics do your organizations track to gauge whether or not you are on mission and advancing your cause? When I was a child, the church I attended had a plaque on the wall listing the songs we were going to sing by page numbers, last week's attendance (on Sunday night, this week's attendance), and last week's offering (on Sunday night, this week's offering). I didn't realize it, but I was programmed to think that at least two-thirds of those metrics revealed whether the church was succeeding.

Staring at last week's attendance figure is like looking at a student's high school report card. When a student gets a "C" in Algebra II, it is too late to change the grade. However, had someone helped him track measurements like how much time he studied, his quizzes and test scores, and what percentage of homework problems he could solve, he would have more likely mastered the subject.

Consequently, his grade would have improved.

Measure what matters, and always take time in a board meeting to review your missional scoreboard.

The Senior Leader Report

The senior leader has taken the time to write a summary covering the highlights (wins and challenges) since the last time the board met. Please pay attention to what she said, ask good questions, and when asked for, provide wise counsel.

Committee Reports

If committees are required to submit reports, give them the same attention and consideration you afford the senior leader. When committees update the board, it is a great way to stay on top of what is happening in and through other organizational stakeholders.

Review the Commitments Made at the Last Meeting

After the last meeting, board members are asked to give their takeaways and state any commitment they have made to perform on behalf of the organization (including a due date by which they will finish the task or tasks). These were highlighted in the pre-meeting packet sent to everyone before the meeting. These must be quickly reviewed to maintain a sense of accountability for members.

Business Agenda Items

The most urgent items should be afforded the most time when comprising the agenda. Every agenda item should have a clear outcome (i.e., is it to be discussed, is a decision required, is a new policy needed, etc.).

In the business portion of the meeting, a board will act most like a jazz ensemble. While different board members play various instruments, people must also be flexible enough to play off each other and improvise. One of the most neglected skills in meetings is active listening.

Make sure in this section to capture in the minutes any motions made (by whom), the seconds to those motions (by whom), the discussions (not necessary to record everything, just the highlights), and the votes taken. This is required.

Commitments and Takeaways

Great songs end big. Too many board meetings just end. You can avoid that by going around the room and having every board member share their key takeaways and verbalize the specific assignments they have committed to completing and by when.

Key takeaways may include insights into issues or problems, highlighting important decisions, reviewing significant strategy shifts, or insights regarding crucial personnel. Takeaways tend to be individualistic and will vary from person to person.

Make personal commitments clear to avoid confusion or ambiguity about who agreed to perform and by what deadline. Clarity regarding obligations leads to better performance and relational health on the board.

Closing Prayer

A closing prayer is not just a courtesy reference to God. It should be more than, "We are in one accord; thank you God, for our board. Amen." I admit, that's pretty cheesy, but

IS A NONPROFIT ORGANIZATION REQUIRED TO USE ROBERT'S RULES of ORDER?

Robert's Rules of Order were published in 1876 nearly one-and-a-half centuries ago. They were written by U.S. Army officer, Henry Martyn Roberts, who became interested in creating an orderly way to run productive meetings when he presided over a church meeting in 1863 in San Francisco. Roberts was involved in the first four of nine editions of The Rules of Order.

Many nonprofit leaders ask, "Are nonprofits legally required to abide by Robert's Rules?" The answer is generally no. However, if you state in your founding documents that you have selected to conduct your meeting using Robert's Rules, you are legally bound to abide by them.

Even if you are not legally bound to apply them, you will find many of the parliamentary procedures very helpful in providing a standardized and orderly way to run your board meetings. The following are just some of the best principles to use:

1. Follow the agenda.

2. Take one issue at a time. Create a meeting flow.

3. One person speaks at a time. Everyone can speak once before a person can speak a second time. Give complete attention to everyone as they speak.

4. Call for the question, make a motion, ask for a second, debate both sides, vote, and record the outcome in the minutes.

5. Use points of order when beneficial.

6. One person, one vote. Officers don't get additional voting power.

7. Refer to Robert's Rules of Order for more details.

a closing prayer should include thanksgiving for what God is doing, a reference to one's belief that he will see you through the difficulties the organization is facing, and a cry of dependence, God will ultimately solve whatever challenges the organization will have.

I often tell leaders going through hard times that I do not believe in the power of prayer. But I believe in the power of the God who answers prayers.

Stage Three: After the Meeting

The closing prayer signals the end of the meeting. But is it? In the next chapter, I will address "the meeting after the meeting." Spoiler alert, it usually begins in the parking lot.

The "after the meeting" stage of the board meeting includes a few simple activities intended to cement the progress made by the board and to maximize every decision and commitment made at the meeting. They include:

- **Sending out the meeting minutes within a week of the meeting.**

  Board members tend to be high-capacity individuals with busier schedules and heavier responsibilities. They have more commitments to keep and more items on daily To-Do lists than the average person. They balance career and family obligations; many nonprofit board members are also active at church. In short, there is a lot of competition for their time.

Getting the minutes to them quickly after the meeting makes it easier for them to stay engaged.

- **Highlighting the Commitments Made and the Due Dates for the Completion of that Task.**

The secretary is responsible for sending the minutes out within a week after the meeting. He or she should highlight each member's commitments and the anticipated completion date.

The board chairperson holds each member accountable for following through on those commitments. That is the difference between a working board and a talking one. You want to serve on a working board.

SOME PRACTICES THAT MAKE MEETINGS BETTER

1. Everybody Listens: Henry Cloud says, "God gave us one mouth and two ears. We need to use them in proportion."

2. Seek Permission to Disagree: We have gotten into the habit of using this question: "Can I push back on that?" It is a respectful way of saying, "I disagree with your point, but it isn't personal."

3. Seek to Understand: Do not assume that everyone agrees without testing what everyone is really saying. Two additional phrases to use during the meeting are:
   - "What I hear you saying is..."
   - "What do you hear me saying?"

4. Everyone Engages: An unspoken opinion is still an opinion. More importantly, it may be a much-needed perspective. Help the quieter team members find and utilize their voices.

A Simple Way to Include God During Meetings

Several years ago, a pastor friend found his church facing a significant financial dilemma. During their monthly board meeting, it was disclosed that revenue was down significantly from a year before. Should the current giving trend continue, the church was facing a shortfall of more than two hundred thousand dollars – a crisis for most congregations, including this one.

The church chairperson was a very successful businessperson. He was independent, disciplined, and averse to running behind budget. From what I was told, he had come to the meeting with his pencil already sharpened. He knew what areas and people he intended to cut.

The pastor confided in me later that the chair had several board members already on his side before the meeting began. The pastor was a close friend. He told me it didn't look good for some staff members – until my friend asked two questions.

He said, "As a congregation, we have been practicing listening to the voice of God. This is either a pretend theoretical exercise or it is the exact spiritual discipline that we need to apply in order to address this challenge. I suggest we table this discussion and take time between this meeting and the next to ask ourselves two questions. The first is, 'What is God saying to us?' In your quiet times and devotions, conversations with other people, and quiet reflection moments, 'What is God saying to you about this particular situation?'

"Then we must determine, 'What is God saying to us as a congregation?' That isn't the second question. It is an extension of the original one."

The chairperson was a committed follower of Jesus. But this kind of spiritual discipline was unfamiliar to him. It made him visibly uncomfortable. But to his credit, he asked, "What's the second question?"

The pastor smiled and said, "After we discern what God is saying to us, we must ask ourselves, 'What are we going to do about it?' The easiest action to take is to cut expenses. But I propose not acting until we can answer those two questions."

A month later, the board reconvened, but they were still waiting for an answer to what the Lord was saying to them. It wasn't for lack of real effort. They weren't ready to commit in a particular direction, especially since God hadn't given them one.

A month later, the answer was revealed. They were to wait. The giving trend hadn't changed. The problem was still dire. One person quipped, "I expected something bigger." She was only half-joking, but her attempted humor did not hide her disappointment. But the word that everyone agreed upon, including the chair, was "Wait." So they did.

I won't go into details, but two months later, one of the pastors decided he was being led to seek another call. He left the church staff, but he and his wife actively remained in the congregation until he received a call to become the associate pastor at another church where he is the lead pastor and leading a thriving ministry.

The giving chart looked like a hockey stick a month after the young pastor left. The church ended its fiscal year with a surplus even though a loss had been anticipated just a few months earlier.

Remember, I don't believe in the power of prayer. But I am confident in the power of the One who answers prayers.

Those two questions can and should be inserted in board discussions more often than they are. Will you sometimes get it wrong? Of course, you will. So start on more minor things and work on the more significant challenges. I once asked my son Colin how YWAM staff members discipled the young leaders and helped them learn to pay attention to and recognize the voice of God. He smiled and said, "Practice and fail. But Dad," he added, "start with little things first." God should be addressed more often in board meetings than in an opening and closing prayer. Don't let your fears restrict your faith.

If you prepare well for the meeting, ensure that each board participant will come ready to engage in the topics and decisions at hand fully, run a crisp meeting, include everyone (especially God), and send out the minutes and reviews personal members' commitments, you will reap the benefits of an engaged board. It will bless your staff and the entire organization.

It is time to address the communication oversight, i.e., Clarifying the Message.

Chapter 11
Meetings and Messaging (Part Two)... Play Who You Are

The single biggest problem in communication is the illusion that it has taken place.

- George Bernard Shaw

Replacing paper with a PC screen doesn't change the need for clear, precise communication.

- Kenneth Roman and Joel Raphaelson

The game of Telephone was fun to play when you were in middle school. The messenger starts with a relatively simple statement, but by the time it has gone halfway around the circle, what is being shared has nothing in common with the original phrase.

Playing a party game when you're thirteen makes for innocent entertainment. But when Telephone becomes a part of board communication, it is no longer funny, and the consequences can damage organizational performance. Bad communication habits are like musicians trying to play a tremendous musical score with their instruments out of tune. Even if listeners can recognize the song, the experience is underwhelming and unsatisfactory.

Some communication from the board to its organization is both exciting and fulfilling. For example, the announcement from Benjie Craig that the congregation had a new lead pastor. Other kinds of communication can be problematic.

A board of directors communicates its mission, goals, and activities to the community, stakeholders, and investors. It also listens to critical feedback that helps to shape strategic direction. It keeps its collective eye on anything threatening organizational unity amongst its members. Musicians have a way of conversing through nonverbal expressions. Jazz musicians are adept at being so attuned to each other that they pick up nonverbal nods or an informative glance about who will take the solo or when it's time to wrap up a song.

Unfortunately, clarifying the message a board wants to deliver after a meeting cannot rely on nonverbal gestures or improvisation. A lot can go awry in board communication. For example...

Board chairpersons can go rogue and independently make decisions for the board without consulting the board as a whole. Chairpersons fire senior leaders, and the board finds out after the fact. Not healthy. Or...

Board members hold "meetings after the meeting" without all members present where they can talk about disagreements and disputes behind other members' backs. Teamwork is destroyed. Or...

Members break confidences. They draw in other people within their organizations and share confidential information. Broken promises poison trust and damage relationships. Ironically, those same confidentiality breakers expect the very people whose confidence they broke to keep their secrets. Trust takes a hit.

The previous three examples are ones I've witnessed. In every scenario, the truth eventually came out (it always does), and each organization's unity and, ultimately, its performance suffered.

Good board members often work tirelessly to develop strategies, adopt policies, oversee finances (including fundraising), and make decisions. Great board members do everything to support, encourage, and resource the senior leader in her leadership duties.

Exceptional boards communicate their actions intentionally and harmoniously with the senior leader. I refer to this oversight responsibility as "messaging." A message refers to the chief idea someone is trying to communicate.

Congruency is crucial to board messaging. The thought of your board communicating something different from one member to another or with its senior leader is the very definition of incongruency.

The One Voice Principle

When a board of directors speaks, it should communicate as if from a single entity or a person. Even if there was debate, disagreement, and division leading up to a decision, the board needs to communicate with members of the organization in solidarity.

The One Voice principle states, "A board of directors should function as one entity, as if it were a single individual.

When the board speaks, it uses one voice, and every member supports decisions even if they did not vote in unison with the majority vote."

Before making decisions, members should be encouraged to share their differing opinions, viewpoints, and perspectives. I am convinced that if sparks of disagreement never fly in a board meeting, inferior decisions are often made. Eugene Peterson translates Proverbs 27:17 this way: "You use steel to sharpen steel, and one friend sharpens another." Allowing one viewpoint to strengthen another perspective is the best way to come to a decision.

Saint Augustine once said, "When two people always agree, one is not needed." When a board always agrees with little disagreement or discussion, it is often a sign that there is a dominant person everyone tends to follow. One person controls the room while the rest of the members in the room use their rubber stamps. When this occurs, members are precariously close to disengaging with each other and the organization's mission.

Disagreements and debates have a significant place in board meetings. They should be welcomed and encouraged before a decision or action is taken. But after the decision has been made, it is time to commit to the agreed-upon direction decided by the board. The concept of "disagree and commit" was created and widely used at Intel. It is used to cheer on disagreement during the decision-making process and to encourage people to weigh in with their divergent opinions, viewpoints, and perspectives. Eventually, a decision must be made; sometimes, individuals can be disappointed when their viewpoints don't win. However, because everyone can freely give their perspectives without judgment or shaming, it is easier to buy in with the plan of action. Hence "disagree and commit" is not as contradictory as it first sounds.

Essential Non-Negotiables of the One Voice Principle

- The board operates as a single entity.

- Recognize that there is a BD and an AD to board decision-making. Disagreements and debate belong BD (Before Decisions), while commitment to implement the board's action AD (After Decisions).

- Post decisions, the board should determine how to best communicate with the key stakeholders in the organization. This is more than posting a redacted version of the meeting minutes posted on a website or emailing them to everyone in the organization.

- The more sensitive or important the message is, the more important it is to share with vested individuals in person.

- After decisions are made, the board determines who is the best person to share the communication (i.e., the board chair, a board member, the senior leader, etc.), with whom it will be shared, and what multiple methodologies (i.e., in person, email, phone call(s), social media posts, etc.) will be used. The "voice" of the board does not always have to be the chairperson or the senior leader.

- Finally, the board should be clear that individual board members, including officers, do not possess any authority to make decisions, communicate board matters, or represent the organization without the expressed permission of the board.

The Oversight of Messaging

Once the board has adopted new strategies, established new policies, changed current ones, or made important decisions, it must communicate these actions to key organizational stakeholders. Not every stakeholder needs to know every decision or action taken. Certain decisions impact only the staff and volunteers. Others impact investors and donors. Still, others impact everyone.

It is essential for the board to take the time to ask the following questions:

- "Who is impacted by this action?"
- "What is the best way to phrase the message?"
- "What method or methods are the best way to deliver the message?"
- "Who should share the message?"

Let's briefly examine the best approach to take to answer each of the above questions.

"WHO IS IMPACTED BY THIS ACTION?" Often, the standard approach to communicating actions taken by the board is to find the easiest way to publish and post a redacted version of the last board meeting. The problem is that people don't generally tune into board minutes like they do their Facebook or Instagram feeds. The minutes are easily ignored if noticed at all.

Not long ago, a board of directors passed budget cuts. Its messaging method was to post the meeting minutes on the message board, both physically in the office and online. The minutes clarified that the 20% cuts were applied to every department within the organization. Everyone saw the message, but one department ignored it, thinking it was not affected. You can imagine the challenges of building alignment and harmony within the organization. The confusion could have been avoided had the senior leader been tasked with informing his leadership team that "every department" did not have an exception clause. It was assumed it would happen, but we all know what "assume" stands for.

"WHAT IS THE BEST WAY TO PHRASE THE MESSAGE?" The wording is important, but it cannot get in the way of making sure that the message being sent is clear and understood by everyone to whom it applies.

"WHAT METHOD OR METHODS ARE THE BEST WAY TO DELIVER THE MESSAGE?" The communication approach is a generation-by-generation and a person-by-person choice. More than ever, organizations must be willing and able to communicate with their audience in a variety of ways, including the following:

- Person-to-person (preferably in-person, online if necessary).
- Email
- Text
- Phone Call
- Posting on Social Media (a variety of sites)
- Website Postings

- Snail Mail (used less and less and for a very good reason)

The more important the message is to the recipient, the more personal the delivery method must be.

Whatever the method, it is more important to adjust it to the one receiving the message than for the messengers to insist that everyone adapt to their preference.

"WHO DELIVERS THE MESSAGE FROM THE BOARD?"

It is important not only what you choose to say and how you deliver it but also who delivers the message on behalf of the board. It is not uncommon for the board chairperson to be the spokesperson on the board's behalf. Occasionally, the senior leader is selected. That choice is best to be a case-by-case decision by the board collectively.

Every message has a particular person, group, or even the entire organization as the primary recipient. Consequently, the best person from the board to be the spokesperson will differ from time to time. The spokesperson will change depending on the best person for that particular message and audience.

For instance, the board chairperson is the right member to deliver the message for important issues impacting the entire organization. If the message affects the staff or volunteers, the senior leader should be the one to share the message. There is a simple rule to abide by: "If the decision impacts the day-to-day operations, then the senior leader should be the spokesperson. But if the message refers to the community at large or key stakeholders or investors, the chairperson would be the preferred spokesperson."

Communication Mistakes to Avoid

When communicating with those in your organization, there are good examples to mimic and bad habits to avoid. Let's go over some of the negative ones to eliminate:

1. Use Email and Text to Communicate Information only!

Email and text are never to be used to deal with emotionally charged topics. And by "never," I mean never!

Never debate issues and never share emotionally charged criticism of someone via written information like email and text. You can never take back a critique of someone or some point you have made public. Do not email or text to correct someone's behavior or performance. Avoid memorializing something negative about a person or group of people that can fester and take on a life of its own until it is corrected.

However, if you praise someone, use email, text, social media, or lease a billboard to spread the word.

2. Avoid the Unauthorized Spokesperson

You would be surprised how often a disgruntled member is willing to speak on behalf of a board without the expressed permission to do so. When it happens, the message is seldom coordinated with the actual message the board desires. It is essential to choose how and who should relay the selected message.

3. Avoid the Unauthorized Message

An unauthorized message begins a lot like one the board approves. It starts with, "The board said... or "The board wants..." I once worked with a nonprofit organization whose board chair was notorious for speaking on behalf of the board. It was not until I joined the board that I fully realized that the chairperson did not receive instructions from the board, as much as he attributed his own desires to their instructions.

4. Avoid the "Meeting After the Meeting."

This toxic gathering often occurs in the parking lot immediately following the official adjournment of the board meeting.

It occurs when one or more members withhold how they really feel about a particular issue to avoid a conflict. You know you have been sucked into a "meeting after the meeting" when someone leads with a statement like, "That is the dumbest decision we've made all year. There is no way I will go along with it." Personal conflict has not been avoided. It has merely been postponed. The friction will likely increase proportionally to the conversations behind peoples' backs.

I once served on a staff where the board chair constantly conflicted with the senior leader. Instead of addressing their differences and resentments, the board chair invited hand-picked board members to meet with him at a restaurant after each board gathering. He shared his opinions regarding the senior leader's management faults. As a result, the senior leader's agenda was constantly sabotaged. It wasn't long before the board chair resigned, only to be followed a short time later by the senior leader. No one won, and the organization suffered needlessly.

5. Avoid Selective Communication

Board members should be cautious and avoid meetings without all members in attendance. Meetings should not occur to allow some members to discuss disagreements with others on the board who are not present at a particular gathering. The initial meeting may be an easier place to talk freely. Still, those types of conversations almost always come to light, and the new difficulty is much more problematic and likely to be relationally painful. Those kinds of meetings result in fractured relationships.

While writing this chapter, this issue arose in an organization I currently consult and coach. A former board member desired to convince the current board to follow his advice regarding a significant decision. When he could not persuade the board to agree with his opinion, he emailed select members or phoned them to gain their support. This healthy board immediately responded by communicating with him and informing him that board members did not keep secrets from each other. Furthermore, they told him they would forward any of his emails addressed to one member to every board member. Finally, they alerted him that the board would function as a single entity and only communicate with him as a group. It has thus far ended his "divide and conquer" attempts.

6. Avoid Triangulation

Often the ugly practice known as triangulation can occur on a board. The disagreement between two board members expands and sides form. Depending on the emotional maturity of the parties involved, it can divide an entire board. The most harmonious boards can fall victim to these types of conflicts.

Jesus promoted "going to your brother in private" as a healthy way to approach personal conflict. People cannot always avoid personal disagreements or disputes, but they can resist the temptation to compound the problem by not addressing the person directly to solve it. Increasing the audience beyond the person involved in the dispute also increases the likelihood of the situation worsening. It also increases the probability that the original disagreement will no longer remain the primary problem. It is best to handle the issue in private.

Messaging is About Communication

It's quite an experience to watch accomplished jazz musicians perform together. One evening Jody and I attended a dinner party hosting two highly skilled horn players from Italy. Both men were members of the life-to-life discipleship ministry known as the Navigators. They were jamming with the other musicians when I noticed Jamie Davis sitting alone and listening intently. I thought, Jamie listens to music so differently from how I do.

I slid over and asked, "Jamie, what are you listening to?"

Jamie smiled and answered, "I am getting to know their personalities. Their performance tells me so much about who they are."

A few months later, I was having coffee with my good friend Tom Patitucci. Tom was our congregation's worship pastor when I was the lead pastor. I told him what Jamie had said to me about the two musicians from Italy.

Tom replied, "Jamie's right, you know. You play who you are."

Tom's comment has stayed with me years later. It explains why even musicians who play the same instrument have unique sounds. Their style is unique or their experience varies. And, each person is a one-of-a-kind, never seen before and never to be experienced again, once in an eternity human being. They sound different because they play who they are.

What about your board of directors? Remember that your board communicates as if it were an individual. Your senior leader, staff, community, volunteers, and investors depend on you to make wise decisions and to communicate those decisions promptly and clearly. Your board communicates who it is.

These last two chapters have been difficult for me to write. I've reviewed basic materials for people likely to be well-versed in these practices. In a way, this is my attempt to model what I've written about communication.

Clarity emphasizes overcommunication instead of assuming that everyone knows what is important. I know you intellectually understand how to plan and run a good meeting. I suspect you agree with the importance of clear messaging to follow through on the board's actions to all the proper stakeholders.

I know you understand. Intellectually that is.

But to *know*, you have to move from understanding to application. If you don't do it, you don't know it.

When musicians play who they are, they let their genuine identity be fully displayed in their performance. When it comes to oversight responsibilities, a board reveals who it is by how they oversee mission implementation, management (especially its senior leader), money, and how they conduct meetings and communicate the results to the rest of the organization. How you perform those responsibilities will determine whether or not those in your organization view you as wise, financially responsible, courageous, inspiring, competent, and caring.

You lead who you are. Where do you want to go?

Section Four
Chemistry

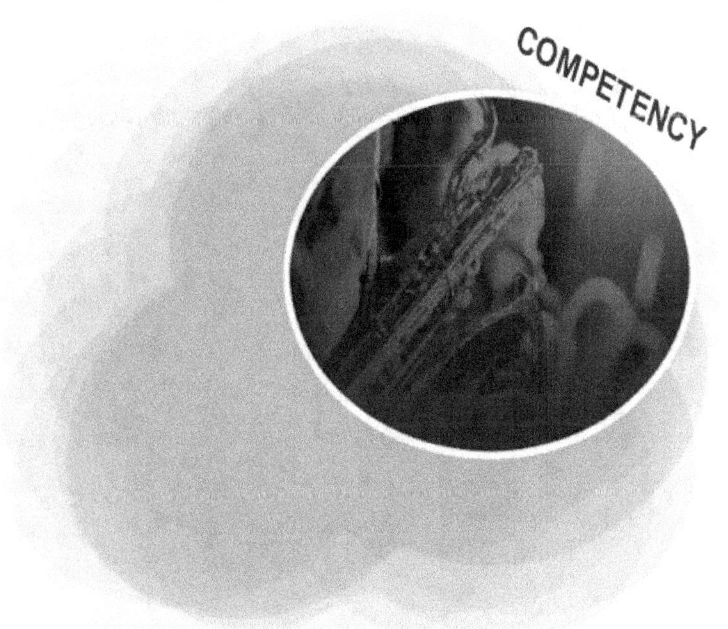

Vibe Eclipse Model

Chapter 12
The Relational Strength of Your Board

An orchestra is the most siloed organization in the world, until it begins to play music.

- Author Unknown

Individual commitment to a group effort: That is what makes a team work, a company work, a society work, a civilization work.

- Vince Lombardi

"IT FELT LIKE DEJA VU ALL over again." The phrase is attributed to the late Yogi Berra. No one knows if Yogi was the first to say it. Many Yogi-isms are misquoted and misassigned to his credit. Nevertheless, the quotation seemed to fit the feelings Jody and I experienced as we walked into the Burbank Music Academy's rehearsal studios for the sixth collaboration between Unity Music and the Count Basie Orchestra. We were there for the two rehearsals leading up to the recording of *Basie Swings the Blues.* It would be historic, blending big-band jazz with legendary blues artists, the vision of Basie's director, Scotty Barnhart.

Over forty people participated in the four rehearsals and recording sessions in the summer of 2022 including music technicians, arrangers, and artists' managers. The musicians and vocalists rehearsed for less than five hours on the first two evenings. On the final two days and in less than six-and-a-half hours, those ultra-professionals recorded thirteen songs. That is what I call "nailing it!"

How does one (even someone as gifted as Scotty Barnhart gather such talent in the music industry, that many egos, and produce what many feel will be a Grammy Award-winning performance? (SPOILER ALERT: THE ALBUM WON THE GRAMMY FOR BEST LARGE JAZZ ENSEMBLE ALBUM! After all, some of the performers hadn't met each other before the first rehearsal, and in some cases, until they walked in to record their particular song.

The explanation exists in one word: Vibe!

There was absolute clarity provided for the artists. Scotty had given everyone detailed music sheets. Each musician was clear about the songs to be performed and how they were to be played. When we observed the first rehearsal, we watched Scotty listen to suggestions and changes from the participating artists. The musicians brought out the best in each other from the very first note played. It was a brilliant way to ensure no one played according to a personal agenda.

The competency and talent level was astounding! Those musicians and vocalists had won every conceivable award (there were multiple Grammy winners, and many artists had already been inducted into various Halls of Fame. One brass player had toured with Frank Sinatra.

Jody and I sat at breakfast the morning after the initial rehearsal with Scotty, Jamie Davis, and executive producer

Sam Beler. We asked Scotty how he could get everyone to perform so well together in such a short period.

Scotty smiled appreciatively. He was pleased that others had noticed how well the musicians had played together.

His answer was succinct. "Of course, all the Basie guys know each other very well. I chose the other artists because I knew they would get along and vibe together." Scotty paused before adding, "When you've reached the professional level that all these people have attained, *the differentiating factor is the quality of relationships in the room.*"

I emphasized Scotty's last remark because it could just as easily apply to more than a recording studio. It could also describe a boardroom.

Clarity and competency are two components of building a fantastic team vibe. The third component is relational chemistry, which is the multiplying or dividing factor of the success of your organization. Great relational strength and health can overcome many challenges your nonprofit organization may face. However, bad relational chemistry is a challenge that not even the presence of terrific clarity and competency can overcome.

There are currently many workplace conversations about building stronger relationships within organizations. Studies demonstrate that those with close friends at work are more productive and less likely to leave their organizations. It will not surprise me if we find out that a critical component of what is being called the "Great Resignation" turns out to be tied to the lack of meaningful relationships in the workplace.

Boardrooms are no different.

After all, people join organizations. They quit toxic people. Dysfunctional relationships anywhere at any time are life-draining.

The Priority of People

The Genesis story informs us that God concluded the end of each of the first five days of creation with "It was good." But when Adam lived and worked in Eden alone, God declared, that "It was not good for man to be alone."

It still isn't.

Relationships matter. Especially to God.

You cannot maintain vibrancy with clarity and competency alone. A board of directors must also possess solid relational chemistry. We do not have to look far to find examples of high-performing visionaries whose companies, nonprofits, or congregations fizzled out or blew up in dysfunctional chaos.

In the music world, we call these "break-up bands." When a band breaks up, it is called "disbanding." In the sports universe, we see the presence of dysfunctional locker rooms. Weak teamwork in the boardroom will generally lead to a lousy vibe, resulting in underperforming boards. Dysfunctional boards place an extra burden on leadership.

People always tell me churches are much better at fostering good relationships than other sectors of our society. If that is so, those same people don't explain why people often get hurt so badly in the church. A friend once told me you could not claim to have been in a real fight until you've been in a church fight. Anything else is a mere scuffle.

Even though relationships matter, nonprofits and church boards often neglect them. From a practical standpoint, boards usually meet monthly. Still, some meet quarterly. Because of the infrequency of meetings and the businesslike atmosphere surrounding the meetings, board members rarely share on a profoundly personal level.

In church settings, board members generally have closer relationships in their small group than with each other. In nonprofit groups, members often have little else in common than their board commitments. The lack of deeper relationships does not pose a problem as long as the organization runs smoothly. But when challenges become pressing, and people's perspectives differ, having personal ties can be a real advantage when conversations require challenging each other's viewpoints and opinions to make the best decisions around critical matters.

A friend once told me that David and Jonathan did not become great friends because they met in a small group once a week. Their historic friendship grew because they knew what it was like to stand back-to-back and wage war together. If you study their relationship, you will see they did not shy away from disagreeing with each other.

The Levels of Relational Strength

Relationships have a stickiness quality to them. On sports teams, certain players are referred to as "glue guys." They are the individuals that help teams develop solid bonds and function together better. Boards also share a particular type of relational glue.

First, there is industrial strength glue. This kind of culture is practically unshakable. Apart from unexpected and exceptional circumstances, these organizations can withstand almost anything. A high level of trust is usually developed from overcoming tough times together. If a board of directors has an industrial-strength glue, the members can likely engage in any conversation, including passionate disagreements and debates. These relationships are characterized by the willingness to listen to each other carefully and respectfully. Board members invite having their perspectives challenged by trusted partners on the board. As a result, there is a high degree of collaboration. These boards tend to make the best decisions because they gather great insights from various people's experiences, knowledge, and perspectives.

Second, some boards possess what I refer to as Elmer's Glue type of strength. I am not disrespecting Elmer's, but it is not as strong as its industrial strength relative. These groups will hold together in good times but cannot withstand the test of more significant problems. This depth of relationships can withstand only so many disagreements or differences.

The third and final type of relational glue is what I refer to as the PostIt Note strength. Post-it Notes glue was designed to detach easily. These types of relationships describe boards whose members are loosely related by the responsibilities they share. The stickiness of the connections will last for about ninety minutes of any board meeting.

If you were to describe the relational strength of your board, would you say your present board is industrial strength, Elmer's Glue, or more like Post-it Note strength? What could be gained by strengthening the relationships on your board – especially when it comes to singing harmony?

The Necessity of Harmony

Most board of directors' meetings are short in length and packed with several business items requiring attention or pressing decisions to be made. Each minute is already spoken for. There is little time for idle chit-chat or small talk.

Relationships might matter, but they often take a backseat to the agenda set before the members at any given board meeting.

The quality of relationships is essential when exercising the oversight responsibilities of a board of directors. A crucial ingredient of any board or team is the presence (or the absence) of harmony.

Harmony, or its first cousin, unity, doesn't happen naturally. Disunity occurs all by itself. Harmony requires intentional effort.

Harmony is an intriguing quality. The Cambridge Dictionary defines it as a "pleasant musical sound *made by different notes* being played or sung at the same time" (emphasis added). Harmony is the outcome of everyone singing or playing a variety of notes.

Another definition is "a situation in which people are peaceful and agree with each other, or when things seem right or suitable together." Harmonious relationships are often synonymous with the lack of disagreement or the absence of conflict.

Far from the absence of disagreements or conflict, harmony is present because people play, sing, or say different sounds, notes, opinions, viewpoints, and perspectives, blended with an overlaying of respect, honor, and understanding. The result is far more compelling than if everyone played the same note or voiced the same idea. A band, a group, a community, or a board of directors experience harmony because of its willingness and ability to listen to each other, play harmoniously, and follow the Holy Spirit's lead.

Much talk is about new, newer, or newest ministry models, visionary leadership, and the need to follow best practices so it is possible to overlook the advantage a team or board has when it is unified.

Trickle-Down Harmony

The biggest reason relational chemistry is so important and is not to be ignored is that relational harmony and unity start at the top of an organization. When it comes to a faith-based organization, the top is almost always the board of directors.

Pay attention to how David describes harmony in Psalm 133:

> *How wonderful, how beautiful, when brothers and sisters get along!*
> - Psalm 133:1 (The Message)

In the passage, we learn how unity begins at the top and works through the entire body of people. I refer to it as "trickle-down." David employs two metaphors. According to David, unity is compared to the flow of the anointing oil that flows from the tip of the High Priest's head, down his beard, and onto the collar of his priestly robe. The second metaphor the King employs is how dew flows from the top of Mount Hermon and down the slopes of Mount Zion. Relational harmony is depicted in the same way. If there is relational harmony at the board level, it is more likely to continue throughout the organization.

I recently completed an engagement with a terrific church congregation that will soon celebrate its 50th birthday. Throughout its history, it has been an essential primary force behind unifying local congregations and nonprofit organizations in a kingdom approach to serving its community.

Like many congregations nearly five decades old, it has experienced some decline in its Sunday attendance, giving, and ministry impact over the years.

Like its congregation, its board has also experienced slumps. When I started collaborating with them, a staff person told me, "There is not a good impression when it comes to our board. We just participated in a churchwide survey, revealing that people's impression of the board is that they are primarily focused on business issues. The impression is that it spends eighty percent of its efforts on money."

While overseeing the financial health of a congregation is a crucial function of what a board does, it can become all-consuming when needs outweigh resources. When economic challenges mount, the easiest way to address them is to make budget cuts. When drastic cuts must be made, it becomes necessary to slash salaries. Entire staff positions may be eliminated.

To my delight, the board did not take the straightforward approach of simply making budget cuts. It reviewed the congregation's purpose, mission, and vision before it took action. Then the members intentionally prayed together and ensured they were aligned in the direction God was leading the church.

They took the time to build a closer relationship with the staff team. They listened to their dreams and understood their challenges. During the Covid pandemic, the board accepted its role in providing solid spiritual leadership. The church is not out of the financial wilderness yet, but it has a strong, responsible financial plan built around the concept that the finances will support the mission God has called the church to implement.

The staff recently invited the board to join them for a fun night at their local Topgolf venue. As the evening was winding down, the lead associate asked to address the group. He repeated the impression that most of the congregation held regarding the board as recently as six months before the fun night out. Then he added, "Our Leadership Team has observed how different this board is. You really love each other and trust each other, and it shows. You have no idea how impactful that is for us as a staff. I can't wait to see what the Lord has for the next chapter in our church's history."

Relational chemistry matters... and it starts at the top and flows down from there.

Chapter 13
The Personal Vibe in the Boardroom

Unity is strength... when there is teamwork and collaboration, wonderful things can be achieved.

- Mattie Stepanek

Many ideas grow better when transplanted into another mind than the one where they sprang up.

- Oliver Wendell Holmes

EVERYONE BRINGS A GREAT vibe into a room. Some when they walk in, and others when they walk out.

The vibe in a boardroom is affected by the combination of the interaction between the personality types comprising the board. When building better relational chemistry on a board, one of the best tools a board can utilize is a personality model that aids everyone in understanding each other and making stronger connections.

Nearly fifty years ago, two cardiologists identified two types of patients in their waiting rooms. According to Dr. Meyer Friedman and Dr. Ray Rosenman, there were two basic types of people. Type A people were high-stressed and driven individuals. Type B personalities were easygoing and less likely to have cardiac problems. This is an oversimplified explanation, but sometimes simple is helpful.

We in our Jazz HeartBeat organization begin most engagement with an executive or leadership team by teaching our signature Personal Vibe™ workshop. This is because the collaborative culture in a boardroom depends on how different people interact. The better people understand each other and connect, the better the interactions. I use our model for three simple reasons:

1. It is simple to teach.
2. It is easy to remember.
3. It is immediately applicable.

The focus of this chapter will not be to take a deep dive into the subject of personalities. Instead of a detailed review of personalities, I will provide a brief overview of our model to apply in a board setting. In addition, let me invite you to visit our website at www.jazzbc.com. You can take a free Personal Vibe™ assessment and find other helpful resources there.

The Purpose of Using Personality Models

The desired outcome of any Personal Vibe™ workshop is to help people adjust to others whose tendencies and preferences differ to create a deeper understanding and more robust connections and maximize collaboration. When team members or board members do this, it leads to better decisions and greater buy-in when implementing those choices.

A secondary purpose behind applying personality models to a group is that it can reduce misunderstandings and avoid or eliminate unnecessary conflicts. People often assign motives (that they cannot see) to other people's behaviors instead of realizing how different personality styles approach situations, decisions, and issues differently.

Personal Vibe™ Types

When learning about personality types, there are endless models to choose from. Some of the more popular ones are Myers-Briggs, DiSC, CliftonStrengths (formerly StrengthFinders), the Enneagram, and the oldest model first described by Hippocrates and later updated by Galen.

Some offer up to sixteen types (Myers-Briggs) or nine (the Enneagram), and when it comes to CliftonStrengths, there are thirty-four different themes or talents to choose from. Personal Vibe™, like DiSC and Hippocrates, describes four basic personality types. (CliftonStrengths summarizes thirty-four talents into four basic types as well.)

Personal Vibe™ aligns closely with the Hippocrates/Galen model and shares similar descriptors with the DiSC or Social Styles profiles. We use jazz terms to describe the four personality styles, which aligns with our consulting and coaching model and also makes each style easier to remember. What follows is a brief descriptive description of each style.

THE PRODUCER: When putting on a concert, making a film, or bringing to life any primary production, the role of the producer is a significant factor in making everything work and getting the result that spells success. Producers are responsible for planning, coordinating, and managing the overall project. They oversee the production's casting, directing, sales, security, finances, and marketing. They don't do it all, but they ensure it all gets done. In short, they are often the boss of everything and responsible for the final product.

Because of their get-stuff-done approach, they can run over others. They hate having their time wasted and must have a sense of control. Please note they don't necessarily have to be in control, but they need to know that somebody is, or they will jump in and grab the reins.

Producers are the Dominance personality of the DiSC profile, the Executing person of the CliftonStrengths, and the Choleric of the Hippocrates-Galen model.

THE PERFORMER: Everyone loves a star performer, whether in a movie, on a stage, or an athletic field. They make everything more enjoyable and often fun. They use their talents to influence the performance of others and the audience. They love to be the center of attention (maybe too much so sometimes), but they bring life and spirit to the team.

They generally have a good sense of humor, love people, and create experiences. Most of all, they enjoy positively influencing other people.

Performers are the Influencing profile of the DiSC model, the Influencing type of the CliftonStrengths profile, and the Sanguine of the Hippocrates-Galen model.

THE ARRANGER: When it comes to a musical performance, the arranger will catch all the production details. Arrangers help rewrite, rework, alter, and improve the final piece. They see anything that might hamper the production because they are sticklers for perfection. They follow processes and procedures and are highly responsible people.

Arrangers are deep thinkers who see things in a framework of steps and processes. They require details before beginning a project, resist spontaneity, and are data-driven thinkers.

Parallels to the Arranger personality include the Conscientiousness of DiSC, the Strategic Thinker of CliftonStrengths, and the Melancholic of the Hippocrates-Galen model.

THE HARMONIZER: These are the relational glue members of any team. They pay attention to the other team members, especially as to how others feel. They are steady and don't need to be the center of attention. In fact, they often hate being the center of attention. They prefer to sing harmony or backup. In doing so, they make everything better. They hate conflict and will avoid it in any way they can.

Parallels to the Harmonizer type include the Steadiness type of DiSC, the Relationship personality of CliftonStrengths, and the Phlegmatic of the Hippocrates-Galen model.

What to Observe in Others

One thing to remember in applying personality models to real-life situations is that people are unpredictable. While an individual might prefer certain choices when faced with a particular problem, one can never merely assume an individual will always make a certain choice.

Personality types have preferences and tendencies. Those preferences and tendencies are not absolutes. Score one for God creating us with free will.

Nevertheless, understanding how certain types behave in certain situations can help groups interact in healthier, more efficient, and more effective ways.

There are three things to observe in other people. Two of them are easy to spot. The last one is more complicated, but practice can help you engage in groups with better results.

The first thing to look for is the person's pace or her outward expressed energy level. Is it fast or slow?

PACING: When observing other people, pay attention to whether they are fast-paced or slow-paced. Fast-paced personalities (the Producer or the Performer) have a certain intensity. They make decisions quicker than most people and bring energy to meetings and team efforts.

Slow-paced personalities (the Arranger or the Harmonizer) don't make decisions before considering the available information and pondering it all. They tend to be deep thinkers and are more detailed oriented.

The second detail to look for is whether a person tends to prioritize accomplishments or relationships before starting a project.

PRIORITIES: When observing other individuals, consider whether they are task-oriented (the Producer and the Arranger) or people-focused (the Performer and the Harmonizer).

Task-oriented people prioritize accomplishing projects or responsibilities before they invest in relationships. It isn't that people are not important to them. They prefer to interact with others on a more personal level after the task is completed.

The personality type that prioritizes people ahead of tasks is the opposite. It isn't that completing assignments is not essential, but they feel investing in relational connection first is more important than getting stuff done.

PRIMARY EMOTIONAL NEEDS: A third thing to learn how to discern in yourself and others is what is the primary emotional need driving their decision-making process. Each personality type has an emotional need.

Here is a quick summary:

Producer: seeks a sense of control and accomplishment.

Performer: aims to influence others and to have fun.

Arranger: wants excellence and order.

Harmonizer: seeks relational peace and harmony.

What to Observe in the Boardroom

Can you see the opportunities for misunderstandings and personality-driven conflicts on your board of directors?

Can you imagine a fast-paced, self-assured, task-oriented board chairperson becoming impatient and frustrated when slow-paced, information-needy, and people-oriented members want more time to process information and consider the impact a board decision will have on people in the organization? In turn, those board members will not appreciate the board chair rushing to another conclusion and expecting them to rubber-stamp the chair's action plan.

Who is wrong in the above scenario? Is it possible that no one is? Is it conceivable they are behaving correctly? They behave differently because they are wired differently. They tend to live at different paces and competing emotional priorities.

Slower-paced personalities tend to catch details that faster-paced individuals might miss. Faster-paced personalities cause slower-paced people to complete tasks and avoid unnecessary delays. Task-oriented people get things done, but people-oriented individuals address the relational health of the organization.

Paying attention and adjusting to slower or faster-paced individuals sitting around the boardroom table is essential. For example, if you are a people-oriented personality type, you need to respect those trying to accomplish essential tasks on behalf of the organization. At all times, you must remind yourself that just like there are various types of people on the board, they also have different primary emotional needs they are trying to fulfill, both for themselves and others.

These differences are why a board of directors needs the strengths of each personality type and the knowledge and ability to help utilize the differences of preferences and tendencies effectively to bring out the best in the overall board performance. Paying attention to everyone and acknowledging their differences is a way to avoid misunderstandings and unnecessary conflict and reap the benefits of the uniqueness of the different people around the board table.

Applications in the Boardroom

The value of a personality model does not lie in the learning of it alone. The value only lies in its application. The refusal to apply knowledge leads to self-delusion and lousy board meetings.

You can do several things to utilize the magical powers accompanying understanding personality differences. The first may be one of the most important when applying this material in a boardroom. It is simply this: *come prepared to every board meeting.*

If you are a slower-paced, deep thinker, someone requiring data and more time to process, don't think you can make up your mind about significant decisions without proper preparation. You must review the agenda of the upcoming meeting and know where you stand on the issues the board will vote on. If you don't have enough information, contact the appropriate board member and get the data before the next meeting.

Essential information needs to be available with enough time to familiarize yourself and prepare on where you stand.

If, however, you are a fast-paced, self-assured individual that doesn't require the same preparation time, you owe it to the more thoughtful members of the board to know why you hold your position. It isn't fair for a deep thinker to accept your gut reasoning behind your decision without explaining to her how you arrived at your conclusion.

Different people take longer or shorter time frames to decide on issues. But when a board only meets monthly (or once a quarter), unnecessary delays result in asking the senior leader and staff to delay executing strategy because the board required more time to make its decision. Or a shoot-from-the-hip type of board can rush staff into implementing plans before people are aligned and ready to go.

A second thing you can do to utilize this information in the boardroom is to *strike a proper balance between acting and caring for people*. The decisions a board makes impact the people who work for the organization and the people with whom the organization works. Fast-paced, get-things-done types of people don't necessarily forget that, but people's feelings can be ignored in pursuit of accomplishment, even if only for a little while. This can lead to an immediate quick win, only to reap disengagement or lack of cooperation later.

The opposite can occur as well. People-centered board members can let their care for an underperforming staff member outweigh the needs of the people said employee's performance is negatively impacting. I have encountered such situations on many occasions.

It isn't easy to balance tasks and people's needs. Sometimes, a board must tilt to one side or the other. It is critical to have a balance on your board and not just one particular personality type.

The last thing you can do when applying personality models in board meetings is to *keep your emotional needs in check*. It is essential to realize what drives our emotional needs. Once you know, it is necessary to know when to control those impulses.

A Producer doesn't always have to be in control or get his way. A Performer needs to beware when she is trying to "hog the spotlight" and be the center of attention. The Harmonizer must be aware when he is acquiescing because he wants to avoid an uncomfortable disagreement instead of leaning in and taking a stance on an issue he knows is critical to the organization's health. And an Arranger must let go of having the perfect solution to a problem and settle for one meeting the need of the senior leader's efforts to advance the organization's mission.

If you are unaware of what drives you to meet your emotional needs, you may become a stumbling block to making the best decisions for the senior leader and organization – not because you are trying to obstruct but because you are working according to your natural wiring.

Our natural wiring has plusses and minuses, unique strengths, and weaknesses. That is why adding the "super" to the "natural" is important when serving as a board member. Don't leave God out of the boardroom!

Don't Leave God Out Between the Opening and Closing Prayers

God in the Boardroom

Relational unity is a huge factor. It plays an essential role in a board's attempt to hear and follow God's voice.

I am a big fan of emotional intelligence. However, there needs to be an element added when applied to a faith-based organization. To leverage emotional intelligence, one must consider four components, including:

- Self-Awareness
- Self-Management
- Social Awareness
- Relational Management

One must be able to identify one's emotions and manage them, especially when such feelings can sidetrack a discussion or damage a relationship while interacting in a group setting.

Furthermore, one must simultaneously be able to "read a room" and be aware of what is happening to the people sitting around the conference table. Then, one must manage all the relational interactions in the room. Emotional intelligence plays a huge role in creating and maintaining healthy relational chemistry.

But when it comes to having discussions at the board level of a faith-based organization, other factors are involved:

- God Awareness
- God Connection

God is often left out of discussions and decisions after the opening prayer. Then we invite God back for the closing prayer as if to say, "Please bless our decisions and plans, Lord." Excluding God is not intentional. Sometimes people forget to ask, "What does God want to say about this issue, this challenge, or this decision."

The Early Church encountered the same problem, but the Apostles were better at including God in their decision-making process. Even the most casual reading of an earlier decision facing the fledging Church reveals God was consulted on the issues. In Acts 15, we read how the Apostles and the Early Church leaders engaged in a spirited debate regarding allowing non-Jewish believers to enter the Church community. One verse stands out as being highly informative:

> *It seemed good to the Holy Spirit and to us to not to burden you with anything beyond the following...*
>
> - Acts 15:28

Luke does not inform us what made Church leaders aware that it "seemed good to the Holy Spirit." Every group of Jesus-followers has to discern that for themselves. We should simply recognize how Early Church leaders were aware of God's presence and depended on connecting with and relying on his guidance.

Unity was a key component when it came to leading the Early Church. It still is when providing oversight in the faith-based world.

Creating and maintaining a terrific vibe depends on more than building healthy relational chemistry alone. Vibe requires the interaction of clarity, competency, and chemistry; each element requires personal attention and development. However, the stronger the unity and alignment are on a team, the more likely the group members will lean in, have honest discussions, and reach more essential decisions and direction.

Russian author Leo Tolstoy once wrote, "All happy families are happy alike; every unhappy family is unhappy in its own way." Similarly, healthy boards are all healthy alike. They share similar characteristics and disciplines. They build a great vibe and enjoy the momentum and accompanying results.

Chapter 14
Chemistry is the Multiplication Factor

No one can whistle a symphony; it takes a whole orchestra to play it.

- H. E. Luccock

Groups of people become high-performing teams to meet a performance goal, not merely because they wanted to be a team.

- adapted from *The Wisdom of Teams* by Jon R. Katzenbach and Douglas K. Smith

I WILL NEVER FORGET walking into San Francisco's Candlestick Park as a nine-year-old boy with the rest of my Little League team. It was my first ever professional sporting event, and I was going to see the San Francisco Giants play the Cincinnati Reds. I was thrilled about seeing Willie Mays play in person. Imagine my delight when he hit a home run. It was everything a nine-year-old could hope for.

But my most vivid memory was not the line drive the "Say Hey Kid" hit. Instead, it was how green the grass was! I was not even sure it was real. Our Little League field was all dirt. Candlestick looked like heaven. (This is the nicest compliment paid to that ballpark in its history.)

Flash forward a lifetime later; this time, I was standing out in the left field area in Oracle Park. It was the relatively new baseball home of the Giants. Jody and I were there to film an introductory video for an event for one of our corporate clients. We called it "Spring Training." It was part of our new management training program.

Jody played a welcome video to kick off the day featuring the Giant's bench coach Ron Wotus. Ron was going to talk about how important it was for veteran players to show up and participate in spring training. Ron's message was that even experienced professionals "never outgrow the basics." Wotus' comment is a good reminder for board members as well.

I had the privilege of performing Ron and his wife Laurie's wedding over thirty years earlier. When Ron agreed to do the video (our client was also a corporate sponsor of the Giants), he asked if we wanted him to be in uniform. When we replied yes, he said we would have to film the piece onsite at the stadium.

That is what I call taking one for the team!

The best part of the sunny day we spent in left field (right under the neon Coca-Cola bottle and the Baseball Glove) was talking baseball with Ron. He is an expert on the subject, having spent over 30 years with the Giants' organization, first as a player and later as one of their longest-tenured and most popular coaches.

Eventually, our conversation got around to the topic of vibe. Vibe may come from jazz music, but it is no stranger to the world of sports. At the time of the taping, the Giants were about to win their third World Series championship in five years. We were curious about how important Ron would perceive relational chemistry compared to physical talent, skills, and overall competency.

Wotus quickly pointed out two critical examples of vibe influencing how the Giants won the championships in 2010 and 2012. He said, "None of the so-called baseball experts said we were the best team on paper in either year that we won. We no longer possessed the lethal bat of Barry Bonds. He retired after the 2007 season. But we picked up key player acquisitions during the season. None of the guys we got in those two championship years was a household name. However, they all performed well and were tremendous personalities that fit the chemistry makeup of the team."

Jody asked, "What stands out most from those two championship teams?"

Ron broke into a big smile as he recounted the pep talk given in the 2012 playoffs by Hunter Pence. "We were down two games to none and facing elimination. If we lost to the Cincinnati Reds that day, we were done.

"Boch (manager Bruce Bochy) tried to give his best version of the 'win one for the Gipper' speech, but it fell flat. Then Hunter added his distinctive touch and picked up where Boch left off."

That was when Pence earned the nickname "Preacher." The Giants rallied to win three straight games over the Reds and later beat the St. Louis Cardinals to make it to the World Series. They swept the Detroit Tigers in four games to win their second championship in three years.

Not long after we spent the afternoon in the AT&T outfield, the Giants picked up a few key players that helped them win again in 2014. Of course, the players have to perform. Having great teammates that get along never ensures a team can win. Otherwise, general managers would trade for cheerleaders instead of players.

Building Vibe

When building a winning sports team, experts ask, "Which comes first? Is it competency or chemistry?" Put another way, does winning precede having a close-knit team, or does relational strength lead to better team performance?

The answer is yes. By yes, I mean that creating and maintaining a great team vibe is not a simple sequential series of chemistry plus competency and clarity to create vibe. The sequence is not as important as having all elements in ample supply.

Producing a winning performance takes simultaneous and intentional focus on all three vibe elements. Sometimes a team rides a long winning streak that leads to a solid, close-knit bond. Another team may leverage its strong relational chemistry to hold the unit together during tough times.

Vibe Leads to Momentum, and Momentum Leads to Results

The next time you watch a sporting event, pay attention to the momentum swings. Vibe is the energy that emerges from the interaction between clarity, competency, and relational chemistry. That energy lives in the atmosphere of a stadium, an arena, or a court. You can watch a team in the competition. The players start to "feel it." They are feeling the vibe, and the vibe leads to momentum. A good vibe picks a team up, while a lousy vibe brings a team down.

One of the ways an opposing coach tries to change the momentum of a game is to call a time-out. This is especially effective in a game like basketball, where you can see the momentum swing back and forth several times during a game.

Board Momentum

Momentum plays a role on a board of directors. Vibrant people make the best board members because they understand the nature of the interaction between knowing the purpose and mission of an organization (clarity), what knowledge and skillset are needed to execute the mission (competency), and the value of possessing solid and healthy relationships (chemistry).

It is essential to acknowledge that momentum has two directions, forward and backward. There is no such thing as "neutral momentum." Organizations can become stagnant.

I want to address how the combination of competency and chemistry affects momentum.

Any team or organization can experience a great vibe when it wins. There was a great vibe at every one of the San Francisco Giants' victory parades following their World Series wins. One might have said, "The vibe was so thick you could peel it off the cable cars." Winning streaks can temporarily hide relational dysfunction.

Eventually, a bad vibe negatively impacts any group of people.

Even a board of directors.

Board Vibe

Boards focusing on the healthy interaction between clarity, competency, and chemistry are at a distinct advantage when supporting their organization's senior leader, paid staff, and volunteers. Surprisingly, there isn't always a big difference between a healthy board and a dysfunctional one. The chart below lists seven characteristics and provides a comparison of healthy boards with unhealthy ones.

Characteristics of...	
...an Unhealthy Board	**...a Healthy Board**
Exists in a mission fog	Sharp, mission-focused
Alignment confusion	Aligned regarding purpose and responsibilities
One individual controls, dominates, or micromanages the board	Everyone is engaged... making decisions together
Perpetuates overreach	Provides oversight
Fudges on roles and responsibilities	Takes fiduciary responsibilities seriously
Controls the senior leader	Resources and encourages the senior leader
Board meetings are uneven... they are like a "practice"	Every board meeting counts... they are like a "playoff game"

As the chart demonstrates, a board can need help building and maintaining a great vibe in various ways. I want to address one specific challenge I have witnessed several times.

I once heard a story about a lead pastor and a board of directors of a new church plant. The pastor was a seasoned leader at several different organizations. He is a well-known author; if I mentioned his name, you would likely recognize him as a popular and respected leader.

A few months into the congregation's life, a few board members informed the pastor that they would be "running the church affairs." All he needed to do was to preach on Sundays and lead a Bible study. This is a perfect example of board members overreaching instead of overseeing the congregation.

The pastor was not intimidated by their power grab. He smiled and calmly replied, "Gentlemen, I tell you what. Let's go before the congregation next Sunday and ask them, 'Who do you think the pastor of this congregation is?'" He glanced around the room and added, "If they say that I am, then I will pass on your offer to run the church."

Over the next few months, and one at a time, those elders resigned from the board. The power play was averted, and the church is a thriving congregation.

Not all senior leaders are strong enough to hold their ground when faced with a similar challenge. Let me add that sort of behavior is wider than board members. I have witnessed it displayed by senior leaders, board officers, and even retired founders of nonprofits or church congregations.

It is time to address one of the biggest threats to board health. Let's talk about how to deal with a domineering personality.

Navigating Strong Personalities

The board of directors is the most influential group in any nonprofit organization or church congregation. Its decisions govern the organization it oversees.

But what happens when a domineering personality overly influences the board? Its performance is likely to become equivalent to the strengths and weaknesses of its most heavy-handed member.

For instance, if the forceful person possesses high emotional intelligence, is experienced and skillful in the organization's affairs, and has capable leadership skills and insights, the benefits to the organization are endless. These leaders usually work collaboratively. Those working closely with them do not describe them as dominant.

It is common for smaller nonprofit boards to be controlled by a single individual, usually the chairperson or an officer, the senior leader, or even by a member who is an expert in a particular field. When this happens, the board can unwittingly become dysfunctional.

A healthy board is comprised of strong, vibrant people who can operate collaboratively, depend on God, and lead with unity and harmony. I want to return to the passage in Acts 15 that describes the decision-making process of the Early Church leaders.

Paul (known at the time as Saul) and Barnabas brought before the Apostles and Jerusalem elders the need to decide whether non-Jewish people could become part of the church.

The decision was complicated because a group of Jews had come from Judea to Antioch and instructed Gentile converts of Paul and Barnabas to convert to Judaism before converting to Christianity. These Jewish leaders are often called Judaizers or those who teach a combination of God's grace and human effort.

The Antioch elders appointed Paul and Barnabas to bring the matter to the Apostles and Church leaders in Jerusalem to make the decision. The personalities in the room was a list of Who's Who of Early Church leaders, including:

- Paul and Barnabas
- Peter, to whom Jesus had given "the keys to the kingdom of heaven"
- The remaining Apostles
- James, the half-brother of Jesus, and the rest of the elders of the Jerusalem church
- The Judaizers

To say these individuals were strong personalities is the definition of "understatement." Let's peek inside the meeting:

> *Then some of the believers who belonged to the party of the Pharisees stood up and said, 'The Gentiles must be circumcised and required to obey the law of Moses.*
>
> *- (Acts 15:5)*

Dominating people love to make demands. The story continues:

> *The Apostles and elders met to consider the question. After much discussion, Peter got up and addressed them...*
>
> - (Acts 15:6, 7a)

The discussion could have been described as "heated" at times. Peter spoke first (read Acts 15: 7b-11). He referred everyone to his experience regarding the conversion of a Gentile centurion and how he and his household had come to faith in Jesus. Peter testified about *what God had done in non-Jewish people's lives to include them in God's family.*

Next, it was Paul and Barnabas' turn to speak (see Acts 15:12). They testified to *what God was currently doing* in the lives of Gentiles in Antioch.

Finally, James spoke about Old Testament scriptures and what they revealed about God's intentions *to make* a place for Gentiles in the Church (see Acts 1 5:13-18). James declared those intentions had come to pass. As a result, he added, "It is my judgment, therefore, that we should not make it difficult for the Gentiles who are turning to God..." (see Acts 15:19-21).

James' "motion" carried, and the Apostles, Jerusalem elders, and the whole Church "decided" to send Paul, Barnabas, along with some of their men, to carry a letter of instruction to Antioch describing how Gentiles were to be allowed to join the Church and what conditions they were to meet (see Acts 15:22-30). In this passage, we read, "It seemed good to the Holy Spirit and to us not to burden you with anything beyond the following requirements: you are to abstain from food sacrificed to idols, from blood from the meat of strangled animals, and from sexual immorality. You will do well to avoid those things."

This was a colossal decision facing the fledging Church. The meeting was full of demands from a group of domineering dissenters. In addition, the personalities in the room were the most influential leaders who dominated the Church then. Their names still have a prominent influence. Yet, with incredible humility, the leaders collaborated with wisdom and guidance from the Holy Spirit to navigate all the challenges.

When the people in Antioch received the letter, "they were glad for its encouraging message" (Acts 15:31). The result was that the mission of Jesus continued to flourish in Antioch and "to the ends of the earth."

Strong personalities were present in the Early Church. But they were filled with humility, openness, wisdom, and the Spirit of God. They led differently. They were dominant personalities, but they did not dominate.

The same can be true in healthy and high-performing boards of directors of faith-based organizations. It leads to a great vibe and oversight of the organizations they govern.

How to Deal with a Domineering Vibe Killer

One would think that if possessing a great vibe was easy, everyone would have it. While it takes intentional actions to build an upbeat vibe, it can be destroyed in a moment.

An unhealthy and dominant personality is the biggest vibe killer and detriment to a high-performing and healthy board. There is no doubt that Peter, Paul, and the rest of the Apostles could be dominating individuals. Your board may have a dominant personality lacking in spiritual and emotional maturity.

How can a board of directors address the founder or senior leader who feels the organization belongs to them? How can a board reel in a dominant board chairperson who feels she deserves additional influence over the organization because of her contribution? How can members redirect the primary fundraiser on the board who believes he is due increased influence on the organization's board? Finally, how does a board address the person who feels they deserve to solely dictate the affairs of the organization simply because they are the smartest person in the room?

These are real issues and must be addressed because the dominant person in the boardroom is plain and simple, the most challenging vibe killer to address.

The most effective way to deal with such a person is to have a respectful, face-to-face conversation directly addressing the consequences of their behavior on the board, the senior leader, and the organization.

How to Have a Deliberate Confrontation

There is no difference between untested unity and no unity at all. To maintain harmony on a board, sometimes, someone must be willing to have what Jody and I call a "deliberate confrontation."

Most people hate conflict. Whenever someone hears the word confrontation, he is apt to imagine an argument, a blowup, or some ugly conflictive situation. However, confrontation means addressing an issue "face-to-face." It does not have to be ugly at all.

At Jazz Business Consulting, we have an entire series of workshops dealing with Deliberate Dialogues covering the skillsets of collaboration, coaching, and confrontation. Let me refer you to our website at www.jazzbc.com to learn more about those offerings. For now, let me give you a few quick action steps you can apply to address the vibe-killing dominant personality.

First, *determine the end result you want to achieve* through this conversation. Decide if and how you want their behavior to change, or even if you want them to continue to serve on the board. If you are unclear about the outcome you want to accomplish, the exchange will likely end badly. Not only will nothing change, but there is also the real possibility that the domineering person will leave with the impression you agree with and support his behavior.

Second, *take the time to "game plan" and rehearse the conversation*. Most corrective or confronting conversations are unsuccessful because people do not adequately prepare to have them. Addressing the consequences of the dominating person deserves more effort than just "winging it."

Third, start the dialogue with, *"The purpose of this conversation is to..."* and then lean in and state what you hope to achieve by having the conversation. I know many people like to frame the "meat" of the conversation between two pieces of bread, better known as compliments. I avoid "Oreo" conversations for three reasons. To begin, this is a corrective conversation. It is better to get straight to the point. Next, you are dealing with a dominant personality, and it is better to get about your business. Finally, nobody likes those conversations, especially a strong, domineering person. Say it straight and stick to the facts, not the feelings.

Fourth, *describe the consequences of the person's behavior* on the organization, the board, and the senior leader. Also, explain his poor behavior's impact on his influence in the organization.

Fifth, *ask for what you want to see happen*. Refrain from hinting around, and refrain from assuming that the other person understands the behavioral change you are seeking. If you do not specifically ask for what you want, you are unlikely to see any difference in the other person's performance or behavior.

Last, *do not assume everything has been understood when you conclude the conversation*. Take time to:

- Review everything you wanted to address.
- Make sure the other person understands what has been covered.
- Ask for the other person's reaction and feedback. Listen intently, but do not wimp out on your request.
- Ask for the other person to tell you what specific changes he is willing to make as a result of the conversation that you have had.

When a particular individual on a board so dominates the organization's direction, it can result in everyone acquiescing to her whims and wants. The result can have severe consequences for the organization's overall health.

Worst of all, it will kill the overall vibe of your board.

Great Teams Outperform Great Players

I will never forget how green the grass was at my first baseball game at Candlestick Park. But I will forever treasure standing out in leftfield with Ron Wotus when he told Jody and me, "None of the so-called baseball experts would have called us the best team on paper," as he explained the importance of getting players that possessed the right relational fit (along with outstanding athletic skills).

The New York Giants moved to San Francisco in 1958, 52 years before they won their first championship in the City by the Bay. Many sensational players like Willie McCovey, Juan Marichal, and Barry Bonds played for teams that never won a World Series.

They were often the best team on paper, but baseball games are not played on paper. After the Giants won their first title in San Francisco, a local newspaper ran an article entitled, "Great Team Does What Former Greats Never Did."

You may not have the best board "on paper," but if you pay attention to building a great vibe, you will create a winning organization. Vibe leads to momentum, and momentum produces results. The kind of results that fulfills the organizational mission!

Section Five
Conclusion

Chapter 15
Encores Are Never Boring!

Cymbal playing is not about how as much as it is about when.

- Saint Anonymous.

There is only one way to succeed in anything... and that is to give it everything.

- Vince Lombardi.

THREE-TIME GRAMMY AWARD winner Hilary Hahn once described a musical concert encore by saying, "The encore is the short piece after the program has finished, where the performer brings out something that the audience doesn't expect." An encore is the equivalent of an extended performance in response to the audience's show of appreciation for the artist's display of talent.

One way to be sure that a musical performance could have created a better vibe is when the audience does not request an encore.

Encores break out in other venues besides just concerts. Instead of asking for another great play, sports fans reward great performances with a raucous standing ovation. Sometimes, people at work can ask a fellow worker to perform an encore in response to an exceptional performance. Being asked to provide an encore is to be taken as a compliment.

Can you ever imagine a time when people from your organization would ask their board to do an encore? What type of board performance would warrant the equivalent of its staff and volunteers to light their Bic lighters, stamp their feet, and cry out, "More! More!"? After all, that is the type of oversight every nonprofit organization or church congregation deserves.

Sometimes it is easy to get caught up in the notion that serving on a board is prestigious. Sometimes it is. Other times it involves a lot of unglamorous types of meetings and the fulfillment of responsibilities unseen by others.

The important tasks a board accomplishes, for the most part, need to be noticed and recognized. Except for the senior leader and a few executive staff members, most staff and volunteers don't pay much attention to board members. They are the unsuspecting recipients of much hard work in a remote conference office or a restaurant's back room.

Every nonprofit and church deserves encore-worthy board performance – not just for large nonprofit organizations or mega-church congregations. Smaller nonprofits and churches deserve them too. Every board's performance matters because every nonprofit organization and church congregation deserves the oversight of a board of directors comprised of vibrant people to ensure its sustainability and maximize the advancement of its mission.

In short, should you choose to serve on a board, do your best to provide oversight that encourages, supports, and resources the senior leader, staff, and volunteers. Don't neglect the care of your investors. Let them know how their financial investments are utilized to advance the organization's mission. Finally, demonstrate in tangible ways that you care about the team and are invested in the organization's cause. When you step away from the board, you will know you have given it everything you had to offer. You won't regret your efforts.

Most importantly, the mission Jesus has for the organization you invested your time, efforts, and finances in will be better off because of your hard work.

Ultimately, the best encore is not a call for another performance. It is not listening to rowdy applause. Instead, it will be one day hearing the words, "Well done, good and faithful servant." Note the words "well done."

Jesus will not say, "Well studied." He will not utter, "Well discussed." Neither will he say, "Well understood," "Well pondered," or "Well agreed upon."

He will say, "Well done!"

Board oversight is something vibrant members do. It will make all the difference in the lives of the staff members and volunteers executing their organization's mission to serve those who count on them.

Spread a good vibe in the world. We discovered the vibe in the world of jazz music. But later, we found it in Scripture too.

Vibe makes for a great rhythm. It works in a family, at work, at school, in a nonprofit organization, or a church congregation. It drives out boredom. Please do not keep it to yourself. Spread it near and far. It will come back to you.

And if you serve on a board of directors, ensure that a great vibe starts in the boardroom and trickles down through the rest of the organization you serve. They deserve it!

You do too!

Appendix A
ABBREVIATED Jazz HeartBeat Board of Directors Assessment

NOTE: The following assessment is a non-scientific set of questions to help gather helpful insights regarding the clarity, competency, and chemistry of your Board of Directors (or Council). Please do not overthink your answers. It is important to answer each question with a top-of-mind answer.

SCORING: Constantly True = 4; Usually True = 3; Infrequently True = 2; Rarely to Never True = 1

The term "Organization" applies to both a Nonprofit Organization and a Church Congregation

1. I understand the purpose that our organization exists to fulfill.

Constantly   Usually   Infrequently   Rarely to Never
True   True   True   True

2. I understand and can express to others the organization's progress toward executing our mission.

Constantly   Usually   Infrequently   Rarely to Never
True   True   True   True

3. Our board functions well, and we genuinely care about each other.

Constantly   Usually   Infrequently   Rarely to Never
True   True   True   True

4. I understand how our organization's mission drives the board's decisions.

Constantly   Usually   Infrequently   Rarely to Never
True   True   True   True

5. Our board supports our Senior Leader (i.e., Executive Director, Senior Pastor, CEO) and believes in where he leads the organization.

Constantly True   Usually True   Infrequently True   Rarely to Never True

6. No person or subgroup of people dominates our board discussions, decisions, or ultimate direction.

Constantly True   Usually True   Infrequently True   Rarely to Never True

7. I understand and can clearly explain our organization's most important priority for the upcoming quarter or year.

Constantly True   Usually True   Infrequently True   Rarely to Never True

8. I know the agenda of our next board meeting will be well enough in advance to prepare and come ready to engage in making decisions that support our mission.

Constantly True   Usually True   Infrequently True   Rarely to Never True

9. When engaging in difficult discussions (content or emotional), our board members lean in and have a spirited debate without personal attacks.

| Constantly True | Usually True | Infrequently True | Rarely to Never True |

10. Board members provide oversight to the Senior Leader and not to other members of the executive staff or the staff in general.

| Constantly True | Usually True | Infrequently True | Rarely to Never True |

11. I understand how to read and interpret our financial statements without additional explanation.

| Constantly True | Usually True | Infrequently True | Rarely to Never True |

12. Once decisions are made, our board speaks with One Voice (as one entity), and disagreements are not discussed outside the board meeting with each other or those outside the board.

| Constantly True | Usually True | Infrequently True | Rarely to Never True |

13. I understand my role as a board member and how to make a personal contribution that helps our organization achieve its stated mission.

Constantly
True

Usually
True

Infrequently
True

Rarely to Never
True

14. New board members are given clear expectations of their roles and responsibilities and an orientation process that allows them to function best.

Constantly
True

Usually
True

Infrequently
True

Rarely to Never
True

15. As board members, we do not interfere with staff or personnel decisions beyond the Senior Leader.

Constantly
True

Usually
True

Infrequently
True

Rarely to Never
True

LAST QUESTION: Would anyone notice if our board did not meet for the next six months? Yes or No?

Scoring Section

Place the score for each question in the score sheet below – using the scoring numbers provided in the introduction:

Clarity	Competency	Chemistry
Is our Board clear about the organization's mission & priority?	Does our Board oversee the correct competency issues?	What is the Relational Strength of our Board?
Question 1 _______	Question 2 _______	Question 3 _______
Question 4 _______	Question 5 _______	Question 6 _______
Question 7 _______	Question 8 _______	Question 9 _______
Question 10 _______	Question 11 _______	Question 12 _______
Question 13 _______	Question 14 _______	Question 15 _______
SCORE _______	SCORE _______	SCORE _______

A total of 18.0 - 20.0 in Each Area = Excellent! Minimal Work Required

A total of 15.5 - 17.0 in Each Area = Some Work Required

A total of 12.0 - 15.0 in Each Area = Considerable Work Required

A Total Less than 12.0 in Each Area = Immediate Work Required

Appendix B
Agreements

NOTE: When governing, providing oversight, and making decisions, what agreements help a board operate at a peak level? The following are agreements around issues that probably are not covered by an organization's founding documents. These suggestions are issues that should be addressed before they arise around a specific incident that forces them to be dealt with.

- **What authority lies within the board, and what authority lies within the senior leader?**

   A governance plan is necessary to organize the congregation/organization to fulfill its God-given mission. Refer to your Bylaws to see what specific authority has been vested with your board.

   Example: "The board's authority is identified in the Constitution and Bylaws and shall not be undermined by the **senior leader**. Board authority is understood to be vested only in the decisions made by the Board as a whole and not in individual members. Therefore, individual members of the Board shall not seek to exercise administrative or individual authority over the **senior leader, staff members, or congregation/organization.** Although final authority resides in the Board, it shall seek to create a relationship of support with the **senior leader** and through the senior leader with the staff as a whole. The board shall seek to support the **senior leader's** ministry, his leadership of staff, as well as the vision, mission, and direction of the congregation/organization."

Example: "The **senior leader** is responsible for casting the vision, forming the mission, and setting the priorities and direction for the congregation/organization. Other senior staff members and Board members are responsible for reviewing and sharpening the vision cast by the **senior leader**, executing that vision and mission, and providing oversight for the care of the congregation/organization."

- **How does your board make decisions?**

  Example: "The Board will make decisions/resolutions by consensus. Consensus is defined as the (Choose one: **vast [ ], which refers to 'the massive or enormous amount' or simple [ ], which refers to a single vote difference**) majority of members being in agreement. If the consensus is not unanimous, members not in accord shall support the decision."

"If issues are not decided upon the first time they are discussed, a period will be set aside for prayer and seeking God's guidance. If consensus is not reached on an issue after __________ **(two or three)** meetings where discussion is held on it, then the matter will be tabled or formally dropped.

Another Example to Consider: "If the Board deems an issue to be unusually critical, the Board can, by a consensus vote, decide that a unanimous vote must decide the particular issue and will not be passed unless there is complete unity and harmony considering the decision."

- **How does your board deal with unresolved issues and relational conflict?**

  Example: "The Board shall address unresolved issues in the church's spirit described in Acts 15 (the Council of Jerusalem). In this manner, there was spirited discussion and debate (and we are convinced that there was much prayer), and the leaders made a crucial decision that shaped the DNA of the church. The leaders concluded, "It seemed good to the Holy Spirit and to us..." Acts 15:28).

"Board members must refrain from meeting privately to create alliances for personal agendas or to gain support for particular issues. This does not mean that Board members cannot discuss issues or ask questions of one another outside of meetings."

"Should a relational conflict arise between Board members or between members and the **senior leader, staff members or fellow board members**, it shall be immediately addressed and not allowed to fester and turn into bitterness, resentment or divineness. Relational conflict resolution will follow the pattern laid out by Jesus in Matthew 5:23-26 and Matthew 18:15-20. Members of the Board are responsible for living out their relationships in a way that models and reflects community within the congregation/ organization outside community as described in the New Testament as the "One Another(s)," i.e., honor one another, accept one another, forgive one another, submit to one another..."

- **How does your board communicate with your congregation/community or staff?**

  Example: "Each Board member individually pledges to engage with members of the staff, the congregation, and the community at large in such a way as to protect the leadership of the **senior leader** and to maintain the unity of the congregation/organization and its staff and the other members of the board. Therefore, Board members will not engage in or encourage inappropriate dialogues or discussions regarding decision-making with others outside the Board. Should there be an issue with the **senior leader**, the Board will address him directly and in person to avoid discord with him or others. When addressing behavioral or performance issues regarding other staff members or volunteers, the Board shall refrain from stepping into an area assigned to the **senior leader**. The Board, however, should address their concerns and desires with the **senior leader**. An individual or group from the congregation/organization should never be able to approach the **senior leader**, other staff, or Board members with the leverage from previously secured individual Board member's support or the leverage of the entire Board."

"When the Board speaks, it will be with One Voice. This means that the Board speaks as one entity and not as individuals. A board member is not to misuse his position and speak individually on any particular issue unless that individual is expressing the opinion of the Board as a whole."

- **How does your board handle confidential communication?**

  Example: "Each Board member pledges wholeheartedly to a sacred trust of confidentiality regarding all discussions. This includes the roles of individual members in contributing to Board decisions and discussions that take place in Board meetings or between Board members and include both verbal and written communications between Board members."

- **How will the board express care for the senior leader?**

  Example: "The Board shall function in a loving and supportive manner with the **senior leader** and will assist him in maintaining proper perspective and priorities regarding his relationship with God, with family, and with the ministry. The Board will help provide counsel and will seek to protect the **senior leader's** time demands and expectations from members of the congregation or organization so that he can focus on the key responsibilities and expectations that the position requires. Any concerns about the senior leader's personal life or ministry will be addressed in person in a loving, discreet, and appropriate manner. Such concerns should never come as a surprise to the **senior leader**."

- **What are the specific roles and responsibilities of the board?**

> **Example:** "The board's primary responsibility, both as individuals and as a whole, is to care for the spiritual health and vitality of the congregation/organization. The Board shall ensure that the mission of the congregation/organization is being executed and that its people are faithfully addressing its achievement. The Board will seek to understand the vision and mission cast and formed by the **senior leader** and will review and sharpen it in partnership with the **senior leader.**"

> "In the case of a church congregation, you may want to include something like the following, "The board shall ensure that the Word of God is being taught faithfully and practically throughout all areas of the church; that people of the church are equipped for ministry and mission; and that worship and the sacraments are a high priority, both in principle and practice."

- **How does your organization manage human resource issues with (A) the senior leader, (B) the staff, and (C) volunteers?**

  Does your congregation/organization have a separate HR department comprising primarily non-Board members, or does your Board also address HR issues? These issues include relational conflict, underperformance or behavioral issues of employees or volunteers, harassment issues (sexual, mental, emotional), hostile environment complaints, employee termination, dealing with poor supervisor/employee relationships, and more.

  If your congregation/organization does not have an HR department, consider contracting to outsource your HR needs.

- **Are specific policies in writing regarding sick leave, family leave, vacation, and what outside opportunities staff can pursue?**

  Should any disputes or problems arise, your board must be informed about what your Employees' Manual says about these issues.

Appendix C
Meeting Legal Requirements

According to the Office Administrator, the group that walked into the entrance to the office wing of the church facility looked like they were all from the movie Men in Black. They wore black suits with white dress shirts and black ties, carried black briefcases, wore Joe Biden look-alike sunglasses.

The group was from the State Franchise Board and came for a surprise visit. They asked to speak to the person who oversaw our finances.

Fortunately for the congregation, that individual was Marvin Schick. Marv was the church's CFO and a long-tenured CPA. He was always on top of the church's finances and kept up with state and federal changes regarding how a nonprofit or church was to operate.

According to the story, Marvin and the men in black from the State Franchise Tax Board met for two hours behind closed doors. At the two-hour mark, they packed up and were on their way out the door. Sandy said as they passed by the Office Administrator's office, "Are you already finished?"

No one said a word.

Then, one man made a U-turn and returned to Sandy's office. He smiled and said, "I have never seen a church with a budget this size in such great shape. I don't think you'll see us again for a while." Then he smiled again and left to join the rest of the team.

The story is legendary in our congregation! But those of us who have had the pleasure of working with Marvin Schick were not surprised. Marv could teach seminars on how a nonprofit organization should operate.

This appendix focuses on how a nonprofit organization's governance should be overseen. It is important to note that the laws of nonprofit organization governance vary from state to state; therefore, it is essential to review your state laws.

Expectations Around Board Governance

When addressing board governance, it is essential to know what it involves and what expectations various government agencies have regarding your state.

Governance describes the process that an organization follows to make informed choices. It involves:

- Why does the organization exist? (Purpose)
- What do you want to achieve? (Mission)
- What are the best ways to achieve those results?
- What are the resources needed?
- How does the organization obtain those resources?
- How does the organization measure the difference that it is making? (missional scoreboard and metrics)

The process includes how the board makes policy decisions, provides strategic leadership, oversees senior leadership performance, and exercises accountability for the organization.

The state and the federal government have expectations regarding how a board of directors governs a nonprofit. Board members must oversee the organization's operations and ensure that the staff and volunteers act legally and ethically.

The corporate structure is put into place to ensure that the by-laws and articles of incorporation are adhered to when it comes to advancing the organization's mission, following the rules and procedures of its operation for decision-making, and overseeing the organization's finances so that they go to fulfilling its intended mission.

Many states use the fiduciary duties of:

- Duty of Care: members show up and actively plan, decide, and oversee the organization's financial health.

- Duty of Loyalty: Board members seek to always act in the organization's best interests and never for their benefit. They avoid conflicts of interest or even the appearance of such.

- Duty of Obedience: board members are faithful to the organization's mission and manage its financial affairs to advance it.

Furthermore, board members must:

- Follow all state and federal regulations regarding nonprofit governance.
- Approves all key contracts and agreements on behalf of the organization
- Attends most board meetings.
- Hires, supervises, resources, evaluates, disciplines, and, if need be, fires senior leader who provides the same for the staff team.
- Monitors and takes responsibility for the organization's financial solvency (sets and evaluates economic policies, approves the budget and significant expenses, and reviews financial reports).

Does A Nonprofit Have to Incorporate?

The simple answer is no. But if you choose not to incorporate, you give up many advantages. Below is a chart that lists the benefits versus the disadvantages of incorporating.

Do You Have to Incorporate	
Advantages to Incorporate	**Disadvantages to Incorporate**
Receive state and federal exemptions for corporate taxes.	It costs time and money to incorporate.
Can receive grants and donations (and donors can receive tax deductions)	Limited political activities.
Can receive in-kind donations.	Depending on the state, it may not be eligible for state or federal programs (separation of church and state); it can be limited to religious activities if it does receive state or federal gifts or programs).
Board members, officials, and employees are protected from personal liability from the organization's debts or lawsuits (NOTE: this does not apply when the law has been broken or board members have failed in their fiduciary duties). The organization must take out Directors and Officers (D & O) Insurance, which protects from the debts or lawsuits filed against the organization).	You are limited to what the organization may pay directors.
You can provide benefits such as health, life insurance, and a pension plan for employees (unincorporated organizations can only sometimes offer these).	When the organization closes, you must give assets to another nonprofit organization.
County and real estate property taxes can be exempt.	
Lower postage rates (i.e., third-class bulk rates)	
Lower advertising rates (radio and television), even free.	
Some discounts provided by some retailers.	

Review Your By-Laws

It is surprising to note how many faith-based organizations ignore the need to provide new board members (or senior members, for that matter) with a copy of their by-laws. Such behavior is neglectful at best and sloppy at worst.

When it comes to meeting the minimum requirements for operating as a nonprofit entity, the following must be adhered to:

- What is the minimum number of board members required? What is the minimum requirement according to the state where you are incorporated? What do your by-laws call for?

- What constitutes a quorum for the meeting?

- How often is the board supposed to meet? (Is it monthly, quarterly, or annually?). What is the state requirement, and what is in your by-laws?

- What is the term for each board member (two or three years)?

- What is the term limit for board members?

- Are board members appointed? If so, by whom?

- Are board members elected? If so, when are elections held? Who votes? How are board members nominated?

- When are officers chosen, and who approves their selection?

- Make sure that board meeting minutes are taken appropriately, including:
  - Name of the organization
  - Date of the meeting, location, and time held.
  - Confirmation that the proper notice of meeting time was given to board members (or that there has been a motion and decision that does not have to occur).
  - Election of board officers by the by-laws and articles of incorporation are posted each year.
  - Meeting minutes always include basic information, and decisions are recorded (including who moved, seconded, and voted for each decision or approval).
- Make sure that the Annual Meeting and Report are recorded. Most states require that an annual report be submitted every other year (check with your state's requirement). The annual report should include the following:
  - The organization's name, location, date, and meeting time.
  - Last year's annual meeting minutes
  - Reports include:
    - Financial Information
      - Year-to-Date actual budget
      - Profit and Loss Statement
      - Balance Sheet

- Senior Leader Report
- Any additional staff or board member reports

Many faith-based organizations make it a practice to post their Annual Reports on their website. It is a great marketing tool to inform the public of your performance per your mission.

Yearly State and Federal Requirements

To maintain its tax-exempt status with the state and federal governments, a nonprofit organization must continue to meet all its legal requirements. This includes:

- Compliance with all financial filing requirements with the IRS and their individual state's Franchise Tax Board, General Attorney's office, and Secretary of State's office. Refer to your state requirements for specific information. Failure to comply will result in the loss of your tax-exempt status. Depending on the size of your budget and assets, the type of forms that you need to file may change.

Board of Directors Onboarding Orientation and Training

The best boards do not leave expectations around board performance to be guessed. They are intentional when explaining the roles, responsibilities, authority, and individual commitments each board member is expected to perform or maintain.'

Too often, new board members are "thrown into the deep part of the pool" and expected to swim with the rest of the team. This is the leading cause of confusion because members are expected to "fill in the blanks" regarding what is required.

Professional baseball players must attend spring training every fall before the start of the new season. These experienced players use the time to get into shape and practice the basics to perform at the level they are expected to reach and maintain. It does not matter if an individual board member is in her initial term or has been on the board for five years; everyone can use a refresher course on what is expected from a contributing member.

Depending on the organization's size and board, faith-based organizations spend an hour to a full day orienting their board for the upcoming year.

Here is a list of suggested subjects to cover during the orientation session:

- The purpose of the board.
- Review the organization's by-laws and provide each board member with a copy and other pertinent founding documents.
- The purpose, vision, and mission of the organization.
- Review the Roles and Responsibilities of board members.
- Review the Authority that board members possess (and what they do not have)
- How the board sets policies and procedures for the organization.
- A verbal report from the Senior Leader, including progress on the current organizational strategic plan.
- The Rhythm of Oversight Responsibilities and how board members are expected to oversee:
  - The Mission of the Organization (One Mission)
    - Review the scoreboard and what metrics are used to evaluate the organization's performance regarding the mission's implementation.
  - The Management of the Organization (One Leader)

- • How does the board resource, support, supervise, and evaluate the senior leader, and how does it avoid getting into the organization's day-to-day operations?
  - The Money of the Organization (One Purpose)
    - • Review the financial statements that will be used at every board meeting
    - • Review board members' responsibilities when it comes to raising funds.
  - The Messaging of the Organization (One Voice)
    - • Reviewing that the board speaks with One Voice and individual members are not to speak for the board without expressed permission and direction from the board.
- • Define what is expected from new board members for the first one hundred days
- • Questions and Answers were provided throughout the orientation session.

Appendix D
Personal Vibe Comparison Chart

<table>
<tr>
<td>

The Performer

DiSC: Influence
CliftonStrengths: Influencing
Social Styles:
Hippocrates/Galen:
Enneagram: n/a
Myers-Briggs: n/a

</td>
<td>

The Producer

DiSC: Dominance
CliftonStrengths: Executing
Social Styles:
Hippocrates/Galen:
Enneagram: n/a
Myers-Briggs: n/a

</td>
</tr>
<tr>
<td>

The Harmonizer

DiSC: Steadiness
CliftonStrengths: Relating
Social Styles:
Hippocrates/Galen:
Enneagram: n/a
Myers-Briggs: n/a

</td>
<td>

The Arranger

DiSC: Conscientious
CliftonStrengths:
Strategic Thinking
Social Styles:
Hippocrates/Galen:
Enneagram: n/a
Myers-Briggs: n/a

</td>
</tr>
</table>

Appendix E
Making Meetings Matter

Pre-Meeting Prep

- **Determine the "Intended Outcomes" resulting from this board meeting.**

- **Design the Board Package, including:**
    - Agenda (include at the top of the agenda in bold type: **"The intended outcomes from this meeting are _________."**)
    - Previous Meeting's Minutes
    - Financial Statements
    - Mission Scoreboard Update (these are the metrics you are tracking to keep up to date on the progress made in advancing your mission)
    - Reports from the Senior Leader and Department Heads
    - Review Previous Meeting Commitments.
    - Add a reminder that everyone must read and come prepared for the meeting.

- **How to Run the Board Meeting**
  - Start with the Check-In: call on each person to share how they are doing. This ensures that nothing is happening in anyone's life that would prohibit them from engaging in the meeting.
  - State the Intended Outcomes of the meeting. Introduce these reports to consider, the issues to discuss, or the decisions to make without commentary or discussion. Say, "Let's begin by going over the Intended Outcomes of this meeting, which are ______________. With that in mind, let us focus on our devotion and opening prayer."
  - Devotion and opening prayer. The prayer can be led by an individual or brief prayers by a few people.
  - Start the agenda portion of the meeting by asking for any edits or corrections of the last meeting's minutes.
    - If there are any corrections or additions, make the changes and ask for someone to make a motion to approve the minutes and for another member to second the motion. Once that has occurred, take a formal vote. It is a legal requirement to record the approval of the minutes of every board meeting and to record this action in the new meeting minutes.
    - If there are no corrections or additions, proceed to move and vote to approve the minutes.

Reports: Next, review the reports prepared for the members.

- Financial Reports: The Secretary should take notes and capture any pertinent discussion regarding the financial reports. After the report(s) have been covered, it is necessary to move, second, and vote to approve the financials. This keeps you in compliance and displays the fiduciary duty of care.

- Missional Scoreboard: To stay up to date regarding the advancement of your organization's mission, review the metrics you have chosen to track. Record the discussion highlights and, if you decide to, move, second, and approve the Missional Scoreboard report. (There is no legal requirement to do so).

- Review the Senior Leader report and the reports of any department leader or anyone else who was asked to prepare one. (This includes any report from any particular committee invited to submit one.)

- Finally, review the commitments made from the last meeting and remind those who made them that they will be called upon to report on the progress made at the appropriate time in the meeting.

- Cover the remaining items in the meeting, including:

  - Discussions of pressing issues that need to be discussed. Be sure to capture the significant comments in the minutes.

  - Decisions that are made always ask for a motion to approve, a second, and record the actual vote of the board.

  - Any other actions that the board needs to take should be addressed.

  - Always remember that there are times when your agenda will not follow the careful script prepared in advance. Remain flexible enough to pivot and address pressing issues that arise.

- After the meeting, go around and ask for take-aways and commitments.

- Close in prayer.

- ONE LAST NOTE: Always make room for prayer and times for seeking God's guidance. One question that is good to consider is this:

  - What is God saying to us now?

  - What are we going to do about it?

You might be surprised to discover how much clarity comes from asking and addressing those two questions. Don't relegate prayer to the opening and closing moments of a meeting. Anyone can request the board to seek God's direction at any time.

After the meeting, send the meeting minutes for review no later than a week. Remember to highlight the commitments made by each board member and the date the task will be accomplished. Sending this out is a helpful reminder for everyone and helps ensure that promises are followed up on and the task is completed.

<table>
<tr><td colspan="2" align="center">Board Agenda
Date of the Meeting</td></tr>
<tr><td align="center">Agenda Item</td><td align="center">Notes</td></tr>
<tr><td>

1. Check-In: "Thank you everyone for being here. Let's go around the room and have everyone share how you are doing and if anything in your life would prohibit you from fully engaging in this meeting."

2. Devotional / Opening Prayer

3. Begin with: "The purpose of this meeting is to…"

4. Review the Agenda: "Is there anything else we need to address?"

5. Review and Approve:

   - Previous Meeting's Minutes
   - Financial Report
   - P & L
   - Year-to-Date Budget
   - Balance Sheet
   - Mission Metrics
   - Senior Leader's Written Report
   - Additional Reports

6. Agenda Items

   - _______________
   - _______________
   - _______________
   - _______________

   ALERT: Do not forget to stop and seek God's direction during the meeting.

   - _______________

7. Takeaways and Commitments: "Let's go around the table and have everyone share one takeaway from this meeting and any commitments you have made to the board during this meeting."

8. Closing Prayer

</td><td></td></tr>
</table>

Appendix F
Board Officers' Job Descriptions

NOTE: What follows is a simple overview of job descriptions of the primary roles that most boards of directors have. Some may vary from your particular board, and terminology may differ, but the following should get you started.

The Role of the Chairperson or President:

- Leads the Board
    - Reviews Vision and Mission Regularly.
    - Proposes policies and procedures to ensure sustainability and continued success of the organization.
    - Creates a system to recruit new board members with an effective onboarding process.
    - Engages board members, staff, and key stakeholders in strategic planning development.
- Plans and Facilitates Board Meetings
- Holds Other Board Members Accountable
    - Leads Senior Leader's annual performance review.

- Reviews board members' performances.

- Usually is the Liaison to the Organization's Senior Leader

  - Supports and resources the senior leader.

The Role of the Vice Chairperson or Vice President

- Will perform all the duties of the Chair/President when they cannot.

- Should the office of Chair/President be vacated, the Vice-Chair/VP shall assume the office.

The Role of the Secretary

- Organizes and schedules invitations for upcoming meetings.

- Records minutes and prepares previous meeting minutes for any upcoming meeting.

- Maintains documentation of all minutes and records.

- Oversees filling out all required forms for the government (State and Federal Tax forms, etc.).

- Personally affixes corporate seal when required for legal or official documents.

The Role of the Treasurer

- Is the lead board member responsible for financial oversight.

  - Maintains cash flow records.

  - Reconciles bank statements.

  - Oversight of income and expenses (and reimbursements).

  - Develop systems to ensure financial solvency.

- Prepares reports for legal filings.

- Creates understandable and helpful financial reports for board meetings.

- Oversees budget preparation (usually to aid the senior leader and the staff team).

- Develop policies (i.e., who can access funds, check signing authority, company credit card use, etc.).

- Oversees organizational audit.

- Chairs the Finance Committee (should one exist).

Appendix G
Board Committees

"For God so loved the world that he didn't send a committee."

- first appeared in a 1959 column written by William Caldwell. Caldwell claimed to be citing a young meeting-fatigued pastor.

"Why are you doing all this, and all by yourself...? This is no way to go about it. You'll burn out... keep a sharp eye out for competent men – men who are incorruptible... They'll be responsible for the everyday work..."

- Jethro, the father-in-law of Moses (Exodus 18, paraphrased).

NOTE: Boards of nonprofits and church congregations utilize committees to help structure and assist the board's work. Committees work best when their expected outcomes, roles, responsibilities, and authority are clearly defined. This includes explaining the limits to their decision-making authority and the clear understanding that they do not possess oversight responsibility of staff members involved in their work.

Not every nonprofit organization or church congregation has standing committees. What follows is a list and brief description of some of the most common committees utilized by nonprofits.

Executive Committee

The Executive Committee is usually comprised of the board officers. In some cases, committee chairs or other designated board members can also be a part of it. This committee typically has the authority to act on behalf of the board between meetings, in emergencies, or to prioritize issues and functions for board members.

Some Executive Committees are granted the authority to act independently of the board. Still, in most cases, this committee must either have prior authorization to act on behalf of the board or have any decisions it makes ratified by the board.

Finance Committee

This committee is responsible for providing oversight guidance on financial matters. It oversees planning, monitoring, and oversight of how the organization uses its economic resources. It will often do the following:

- Develop a budget for how the organization allocates its funds.
- Advises the board on the development of financial policies.

- Oversees and reviews the organization's independent audit (unless an Audit Committee exists).
- Advises the board on matters relating to insurance policies and investments.
- Reviews and manages financial statements, account reconciliation, financial records, and everything else concerning finances.
- Anticipates financial problems.

Fundraising Committee

This committee provides guidance, support, and oversight to all significant forms of investor development and planning of raising capital and operating funds to ensure the organization can implement its mission. This committee typically works with the staff and board to organize and execute its fundraising events and efforts, including soliciting gifts from major donors and foundation grants.

Nominating Committee

This committee is sometimes referred to as the Governance Committee. It takes on the essential role of board development by addressing the following responsibilities:

- Recruiting prospective board members.

- Onboarding new board members.
- Educating current board members regarding the expectations and responsibilities that they carry in their role.

In some organizations, this committee evaluates the board and leads members to self-assess their performance. In rare instances, this committee nominates board officers.

Personnel Committee

The Personnel Committee typically oversees the planning and monitoring the organization's use of its people resources, paid staff, and volunteers. It develops human resource policies and addresses issues like:

- Job performance
- Management and supervision
- Compensation and benefits
- Dealing with grievances
- Underperforming and misbehaving employees.

In some cases, the annual evaluation of the senior leader is led by this committee.

Marketing Committee
(or Public Relations Committee)

This committee often works hand in hand with the fundraising committee. It concerns itself with branding the organization. It is equally focused on internal marketing (communication with the organization's stakeholders) and external marketing (outward-facing and communicating with city and community officials, potential investors, and its intended target community). The organization's internal and external audiences must be educated as to the mission and activities it is concentrated on implementing. This committee promotes events, manages social media platforms, and creates brochures, flyers, and even whitepapers.

Some nonprofit organizations have a Public Relations Committee that manages many of those activities, but it isn't uncommon to combine them.

Other Committees

Depending on the size and specific needs of the organization, nonprofits can utilize several other committees, including the Building Committee, Audit Committee, Membership Committee, Board Statutory Committee, Communications Committee, Policy Development Committee, etc. Is it any wonder that William Caldwell quoted the exhausted young pastor as saying, "For God so loved the world that he didn't send a committee!"

The Three-Committee Approach

Some nonprofits and churches have adopted a simplified approach to committees. It is referred to as the Three-Committee Model. Instead of having several standing committees, a board has three strategic committees designed to help it cover its fiduciary duties. The three committees are:

- The Governance Committee
- The Internal Committee
- The External Committee

The board can identify individuals who possess particular strengths, spiritual gifts, and life experiences that would be helpful in one of the three committees. Each committee carries several different responsibilities that are listed in the model below:

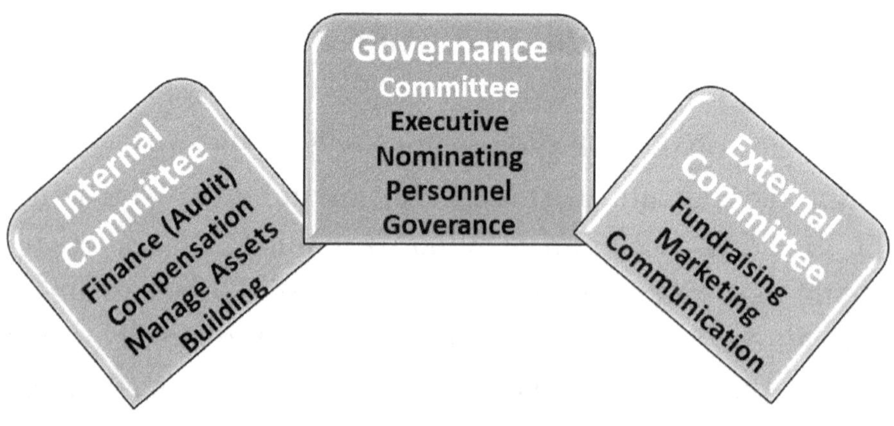

When it comes to a church's or nonprofit organization's committee structure, the critical choice is to create committees that function in a way that supports the work of its board. This means that the committee's work is essential to advancing the organization's mission and that competent men and women are in a place where their gifts, experiences, wisdom, and competency can benefit everyone.

Appendix H
Life Stages of a Board of Directors

Not all boards of directors are the same. They do not fit one size or one function. Some board members must get more involved in the day-to-day operations because of the financial constraints that the organization is facing. Some organizations have to "crawl" before they can "walk" or walk before they can "run." Some organizations have gotten so big that the board is in "cruise mode."

An organization can go through three simple stages, but it does not necessarily have to. As the organization passes through these stages, the requirements and responsibilities of a board of directors will shift and change.

The Launch Stage

Not every start-up faith-based organization can afford to rent an office or meeting space or even pay the senior leader. Think of Steve Jobs and Steve Wozniak starting Apple Computers in a garage. Many faith-based organizations reflect on their humble beginnings and "wish they had a garage."

In the launch stage of an organization, there are tendencies (not rules!) that the board follows, including:

- It is possible, sometimes even likely, that the board will follow the founder or chairperson. The two may even be the same individual. This is somewhat natural because this individual will probably understand the organization's purpose, vision, and mission better than anyone else.

- The board tends to be small initially, likely consisting of three to five people.

- The board takes on more of a leadership role, and it feels like they control the organization. It feels that way because it likely does.

- The board may be slow in initially hiring staff and expanding the organization.

- Problems that the launch stage organization may run into include:
  - Finances, as in not enough money.
  - Donor base development is slow initially because the message is usually more "sizzle than substance."
  - Expectations are unclear regarding how the board will function initially and then change as the organization grows.
  - New members have varying expectations.
  - Personal conflict between staff and the board can arise as individuals try to align the organization's direction.

- Making everyone aware of what the mission is and is not.

- As the organization grows, some board members may be reluctant to give up day-to-day responsibilities and control of the organization.

The launch phase board is often made up of people who are more concerned with getting things done than providing oversight for the organization.

The Oversight/Governing Stage

In this organizational stage, the board begins to fulfill its primary oversight responsibilities and is less involved in day-to-day operations. The board oversees mission, management, money, and messaging. It focuses on policies, organization contracts, significant purchases, and strategic planning.

Instead of running the organization, the board concentrates on supporting, supervising, evaluating, and resourcing the senior leader so that they can lead the organization in executing its mission.

The board's tendencies during this stage include:

- It will likely grow in size.

- It will become more involved in fundraising.

- It will take on a greater representation of the organization in the community.

- It will be more experienced and nuanced in implementing its duties and responsibilities.

The Institutional Stage

Most board responsibilities are likely delegated to an Executive Committee at the institutional stage. The organization has grown in size and finances, and its history makes it easier to recruit and fundraise.

Tendencies during this stage include:

- The board becomes large.
- A board member's role mainly becomes financial, including personal contribution and fundraising.
- The entire board seldom meets together, perhaps limited to the Annual Meeting.
- The organization has an extensive, experienced, and well-developed staff. The staff can conduct all of the day-to-day operational duties of the organization.

It is important to repeat that not every board of directors will go through all three development phases. Many boards jump into Phase Two and begin governing right away. Some organizations take longer to grow out of the launch phase; therefore, the board stays deeply involved in the organization's daily responsibilities.

When determining how a board should operate, it is important to consider the organization's current phase and adjust to meet the needs of the faith-based organization's current situation.

Appendix I
The Difference Between a Church and a Nonprofit Board

This appendix does not settle the argument about which type of ecclesiastical government is the most Biblical or the best. While board governance for a nonprofit organization is pretty straightforward, the same cannot be said for church governance. It isn't easy to know where to start this discussion. You'll soon see why I did not include this topic in the central part of the book. When discussing church governance, one must know what particular model you are discussing.

There are three main categories of church governance: episcopal, presbyterian, and congregational. The first two are pretty straightforward, but congregational churches have many different idiosyncrasies to choose from when determining a particular style of church governance.

The Difference Between a Church and a Christian Nonprofit Organization

Let's begin with the simple distinctions between a church and a nonprofit organization. When differentiating between a church and a nonprofit organization, a church's spiritual and worship elements stand out. Churches are distinguished in having an established place of worship, a congregation, a creed, an ecclesiastical government, and regular worship services.

A religious or Christian nonprofit organization is distinguished by its public declaration of faith and stated purpose and mission. This declaration is found in the incorporation articles and by-laws it files when seeking nonprofit status with its state and the IRS. It should also appear on its website, social media platforms, and any collateral pieces it produces. Christian nonprofits do not regularly hold worship gatherings involving a particular congregation.

There are legal differences between a church and a nonprofit organization. For instance, churches are typically exempt from some state and federal legal requirements about Christian nonprofits. A church is automatically recognized as exempt and need not apply to the IRS, while a Christian nonprofit must apply to the IRS for exempt status.

Nonprofit and Congregation Differences

There is no one-size-fits-all answer regarding how a local congregation is governed compared with a nonprofit organization. Some church board governance looks precisely like its church congregation counterpart. You wouldn't notice any significant differences between the two. However, depending on the congregation's denomination, the differences between board governance can be significantly different, even from other churches.

Qualifications for Governance Offices

Let's start with what qualifications a church looks for in its board offices versus that of a Christian nonprofit. To be a bishop, elder, or deacon in a church congregation, clearly defined qualifications are described in the New Testament letters that must be met to serve in one of those offices. These qualifications include being above reproach, self-controlled, respectable, able to teach, a role model as a spouse and parent, not a recent convert, not in love with money, to mention a few that the Apostle Paul lists in I Timothy 3 and Titus 1. These are must-have qualities, not mere suggestions.

When considered for a Christian nonprofit board position, some of the same qualities may be desired, while others would not. For instance, it is unlikely that someone would be disqualified as a board candidate because they could not teach the Bible to others, and neither would they be expected to "pray for the sick." Some have spiritual and doctrinal aptitudes that are must-haves in a congregation but are not required to be on a nonprofit board, even one distinctly Christian.

Instead, a nonprofit organization is likely to look for qualities such as the candidate's professional background and experience, their professional and personal network, the ability to work with high-capacity individuals, and (in complete honesty), in many instances it is the ability to raise or provide money for the organization. Rarely is a nonprofit board seeking someone with deep doctrinal knowledge.

The Three Types of Church Governance

One crucial issue arises when describing how a church board (or council, session, vestry, etc.) oversees its congregation. What form of ecclesiastical governance is one describing?

There are three forms of church government. They are episcopal, presbyterian, and congregational. What follows is a very brief overview of each one.

EPISCOPAL: this form of governance is hierarchical. Bishops hold significant authority in leadership and decision-making. The local clergy and laity may possess degrees of input regarding the four components of the Rhythm of Oversight described in the body of this book; the ultimate authority resides with the office of bishop (from the Diocese to the Archbishop).

PRESBYTERIAN: leadership in this form of church governance rests in the elected bodies of elders, referred to as presbyters. Congregations are led by elders elected by their congregations and the teaching elder (pastor), who comprise the regional presbyteries. These bodies are called sessions, presbyteries, synods, and the General Assembly. Like the episcopal, this form is hierarchical, and leadership and decision-making authority on particular matters come from the top down. However, the local congregational session has significant decision-making ability for its congregation.

CONGREGATIONAL: in this form of church governance, the authority to govern a local congregation typically, but not always, resides with the congregation itself. While elders, and sometimes deacons and trustees, may be elected by church members and provided limited leadership authority and decision-making, the final authority on critical matters must have local congregational membership approval. These issues may include passing the annual budget, key land purchases, building projects, calling the lead or particular associate pastors, etc.

Other types of congregational governance exist. One case is what is called single elder or single pastor governance. In this instance, the church's by-laws provide decision-making authority to the lead pastor (frequently the congregation's founder). This particular form of government allows quick decisions and single-minded direction to be declared, but the absence of accountability creates potential threats and challenges. Should that "single leader" make unwise decisions or experience moral failure, the consequences can devastate the entire congregation.

Again, this is a simplistic overview of the three typical forms of church governance. What is significant is the way a church congregation's equivalent to a board follows its by-laws and applies its particular form when leading its members and making meaningful decisions that will execute its mission.

Church Governance and the Rhythm of Oversight

Stop for a moment to consider that there are over 300,000 church congregations in America. Particular congregations undoubtedly implement their form of governance in various ways. A simple chart shows how a congregation's Rhythm of Oversight responsibilities are carried out under the three different forms of governance.

Church Governance & the Rhythm of Oversight Review		
Who Oversees	**Episcopal**	**Presbyterian**
Mission	Bishops	The Session (includes Senior Pastor)
Management (Minister)	Diocese Bishop	The Session
Money	Bishop or Diocesan Structure (i.e., Treasurer, Committee, etc.)	The Session (approves budget, manages financial matters, aligns with Presbyterian polity)
Messaging (Communication)	Bishop	The Moderator of the Session
What Authority Does the Lead Minister Have?	Bishops are at the top of the hierarchical ladder	The Session has final authority in decision-making but often shares with the pastor, who is a member of the Session)
Types of Churches Include:	Episcopal, Easter Orthodox, Copic, Roman Catholic, Anglican, Methodist, and some Lutheran.	Presbyterians, Reformed

Church Governance & the Rhythm of Oversight Review

Who Oversees	Democratic Congregational	Congregational Single Led Elder or Pastor	Congregational Elected Elder Board (and perhaps Deacons and Trustees)
Mission	Elected Leaders with Congregational Approval	The Lead Pastor (who may lead like a CEO)	Elders with Congregational Approval
Management (Minister)	Elders	No Accountability	Elders
Money	Elders, Elected Trustees, Finance, Committee, Congregational Approval	The Lead Pastor (may delegate)	Elders, Elected Trustees, Finance Committee (all with Congregational Approval)
Messaging (Communication)	Usually through the Elder Board or Lead Pastor	The Lead Pastor	Usually through the Elder Chair of Lead Pastor
What Authority Does the Minister Have?	Primarily seen as the spiritual leader and preacher/teacher.	Has Full Control	Primarily seen as spiritual leaders and preacher/teacher.
Types of Churches Include	Baptists, Evangelical Free, Evangelical Covenant, Pentecostal, Charismatic, Some Lutheran, and other Congregational Churches		

LEARN MORE ABOUT WHAT
JAZZ HEARTBEAT HAS TO OFFER

Every nonprofit organization and church congregation deserves the oversight of a board of directors comprised of vibrant leaders to ensure its sustainability and maximize the advancement of its mission.

In turn...

Every nonprofit or church board member deserves clarity about what is expected of them, their roles and responsibilities, and training so they can succeed.

We make it simple:

TALK TO A COACH	CHOOSE AN ASSESSMENT OR A TAILORED TRAINING OR COACHING ENGAGEMENT	MAKE AN IMPACT IN YOUR COMMUNITY

Contact us at www.heartbeat.org or call 888.938.JAZZ (5299)

Board Development Book Reviews

Roger Dill has extensive real-life experience with boards. He has served on, led, advised, and consulted numerous ones. His book is a powerful collection of practical applications and extremely effective tools. His candid, personal vulnerability establishes instant trust with his audience, who know that he will say what needs to be said when it needs to be said.

Board Development is a great toolbox, and it includes the book, assessments, and consulting to drive board effectiveness and mission success! If you have a Board or are on a Board, this is the one tool you want to make sure is being utilized. Do not attend another Board meeting without it!

Neil Sullivan Principal Consultant, The Table Group, and President and CEO of The Leadership Connection

Roger Dill's new book, "Board Development," is essential for anyone involved in church leadership. Focusing on maximizing the impact of a church's board, Dill emphasizes the importance of clarity, competency, and chemistry. His practical insights and highly recommended "board assessment tool" make this book a valuable resource for fostering dynamic board governance. "Board Development" is a guide for any church looking to enhance the effectiveness of its board. It belongs in every pastor's library and utilized by every church board.

Bernard Emerson, Regional President Converge PacWest

I received an advanced copy of Roger Dill's book, Board Development, and it came at just the right time. Our congregation's senior pastor was called to another church at the same time that our business manager and administrator were both retiring. Our board had a heightened sense of urgency to address three key hiring decisions during the transition period when giving generally dropped significantly. I needed a concrete director. Then I read Roger's advice to "do away with donors and turn them into investors." That was a mic-drop moment for me. Across the page, I read, "The board is responsible for ensuring that the organization puts its money where its mission is." This book is full of spot-on advice that is applicable to rookie board members and experienced veterans alike. I also lead a business and will use many of the nuggets and exercises to advance our "why." Board Development is for you if you want an easy read that will get you thinking about how to lead better.

Lisa Carter, Vice President of CD & Power Company and Chair of Resurrections Ministries

Dedication

For Jody,

This work would never have been completed without your consistent encouragement and dedication to our present and future. You refuse to settle for anything less than giving your best and inspire others and me to do the same.

For Colin (and Jess, Finleigh, and Rowan), Cameron, Grace (and Tyler), and Sam,

You all embody our future, and it shines with hope and promise. As Jesus said, "God loves a cheerful giver." You have given the best gift to others by first giving of yourselves, and I am confident that your future is filled with even greater achievements and contributions.

Acknowledgments

This book may list my name as its author, but it is far from a solo project. My wife and business partner, Jody Bagno-Dill, deserves so much credit. I wouldn't think about writing anything, such as a book, a blog, a workshop, or a sermon, without her reviewing it and giving me feedback. Her counsel is wise, and her wit is unequaled. You, the readers, have been spared long-winded stories simply because Jody was willing to ask, "Is that the best way to communicate that particular idea?" I know most authors refrain from mentioning their spouse's contribution until the end of the acknowledgments section, but I wanted to start with the human being most responsible for making this a better book!

Next is our executive assistant Hava Kimmel-Miner. Hava recently celebrated ten years with our company, and Jody and I would be lost without her. She is a master organizer, which is not always easy when she is trying to herd two expressive personalities. If your nonprofit or church congregation should ever choose to use one of our assessments, you can thank Hava in advance for getting each of them over the end line. We count on her to have our backs and ensure that the clients we serve are expertly cared for.

The team at The Paper House played a crucial role in bringing this book to life. My project manager, Mike Rizk, guided me through the process with patience and professionalism, never making me feel like a rookie author. My editor, Art Fogartie, was insightful and helpful. I learned a lot about saying things in a simple way. Their collective effort and support have made this book a reality.

God had his hand on me in many ways as I meandered through college and my early days in the nonprofit world. John Price was the executive director at the YMCA, where I first learned about leadership, fundraising, and what it meant to be a part of a team. Mr. Price saw something in me and hired me as the summer lifeguard. I never told him that I couldn't swim. (The pool was only six feet deep!) His successor, Roger Griffing, taught me how to take working in a nonprofit to a professional level. He raised my game significantly.

Mr. Price allowed me to lead the teen program at the Y. I convinced him to let me raise enough money to hire an assistant. His name was Lon Allison. Lon and I became lifelong friends. He even returned the act by hiring me as his associate pastor at a church he had started. Lon went on to become the Executive Director at the Billy Graham Center of Evangelism on the Wheaton College campus. Lon's friendship was a cornerstone of my early maturing as a man. Lon passed away four years ago, and I miss him deeply. Lon wasn't the only friend to whom I owe so much gratitude. My personal character was deeply impacted by other friends I met at the Y like Kevin Morgan, Mike Lippman, Neil Sullivan, and John Eklund.

After leaving the YMCA, I joined the staff of Youth for Christ in the San Francisco Bay Area. Larry Weins, Don Mardock, Ted Smith, and Roger Cross mentored me, to mention only a few. I made many friends during my years in YFC and count my friendships with Bill Muir, Jerry Hanson, and Samy D'Amico as life-altering.

The broader church (and some specific congregations) is a whole other world full of transformative friendships. Pastors Jim Persson and Tom Collins were instrumental in my spiritual growth and as a leader. I have always had incredible ministry partners. I count Tom and Karen Patitucci, Karen Cadle, Theresa Kukla, and Steve Anderson on that list (others have already been mentioned).

I want to say thank you to all the partnering leaders in the Leadership Connection groups I have had the privilege to facilitate. It was my joy to grow along with you all!

This list wouldn't be complete without acknowledging some of the board chairs I have learned from over the years. To Bob Jones, Scott Walker, Ron Knapp, Benjie Craig, and Russell Adams, please know how much I have learned from you all! You have shaped the positive nature of this book. Without your impact on my life, it would never have been written.

A special recognition goes out to Gary Depolo. Gary, you are the finest example of what is best about nonprofit board members. You are wise, generous, insightful, and fearless. You are what I aspire to become.

I have mentioned many lifetime friendships that have shaped who I am. Lon, Steve, Tom, Karen, Ron, Karen, Bob, Jerry, and Kevin—the good parts of me reflect your impact on my life. (The work still in progress is all on me.) Add friends like Bert and Mary Norcross, Doug Stevens, Kevin

Murphy, Dave and Gina Blok, Dr. Mitch Applegate, and Sam Beler to this list. You have seen me at my worst but loved me nonetheless. We have laughed together, cried tears, bemoaned losses, and celebrated wins. This thing called life is made rich because of people like you!

Our kids are the best! Each one is different. Really different! You have made life an adventure, at times, a comedy, and even an action thriller. It has never been boring. You have all decided to pursue your own career paths, and we couldn't be prouder of you and who you have become. Adding Jess, Finleigh, Rowan, and Tyler to our family has multiplied our family's variety, richness, and fun. Your best years are ahead of you, and we can't wait to see how you shape the world around you.

Parents never get the credit and acknowledgment that they deserve. I am fortunate to be one of those individuals who adore his in-laws. My parents have been gone for a long time. I am grateful to my dad for modeling the relational skills that he did and to my mom for instilling in me the disdain for settling for less than excellence. My sister is so kind and warm that she makes Mother Thersa appear mean. To Lloyd, Neva, Zoe, Barbara, Larry, and Harry, I hope you are aware of my love and gratitude for all of you. Special recognition goes to my aunt and uncle Doyle and Florene, who were like a second set of parents, grandparents, and older siblings all wrapped together in a bundle of life-giving energy and love.

Mentioned last, but who is first in my life is Jesus. I realize that any good ideas have come from you. I depend on you for every breath. I recognize that every good and every perfect gift comes from you. I recognize that anything from me that blesses others is from you. I want to represent you well and bring a smile to your face.